Becoming Financially Fit

"No one's ever achieved financial fitness with a January resolution that's abandoned by February."
-Suze Orman

"The ability to discipline yourself to delay gratification in the short term in order to enjoy greater rewards in the long term is the indispensable prerequisite for success."
-Brian Tracy

"There is no path to happiness; happiness is the path."
-Gautama Buddha

"Integrity is choosing courage over comfort."
-Brené Brown

"The reason I've been so financially successful is my focus has never, even for one minute been money."
-Oprah

FINANCIALLY FIT

Living the Secrets to an Abundant and Prosperous Life

DAWNA CAMPBELL

BEYOND
PUBLISHING

Quantity sales special discounts are available on quantity purchases by corporations, associations, and others. For details, contact the publisher at the address above.

Orders by U.S. trade bookstores and wholesalers. Email info@BeyondPublishing.net

The Beyond Publishing Speakers Bureau can bring authors to your live event. For more information or to book an event contact the Beyond Publishing Speakers Bureau speak@BeyondPublishing.net

The Author can be reached directly at BeyondPublishing.net

Manufactured and printed in the United States of America distributed globally by BeyondPublishing.net

BEYOND
PUBLISHING

New York | Los Angeles | London | Sydney

ISBN Hardcover: 978-1-637920-40-4

ISBN Softcover: 978-1-637920-09-1

TABLE OF CONTENTS

Dedication

For my children,
Matthew, Anna Marie, and Aubrianna.
Without you, I wouldn't be.
Thank you for being my silver lining in this world.

Words are sometimes hard to express for all the love, support, and kindness that I have received while writing *Financially Fit*. Without you, *Financially Fit* would not have been a reality. Heartfelt gratitude for Laurén Laurino and Jason Antalek for starting me on this journey. Jill Lublin, much love to you for your guidance and expertise. Your encouragement in moving forward and "getting it done" is truly priceless. David Fagan, your abilities to wordsmith, edit, coach, and guide are truly one-of-a-kind, and I have been blessed to have had the opportunity to work with you. A huge thank you to Bob Macko, of Lux-Productions, for an amazing book cover, websites, and graphic designs. Special thanks to Janet Melody for my last-minute graphics and Michelle Calloway, of Revealio, for allowing the book cover to "come alive". Thank you Beyond Publishing and Michael Butler for the support that you provided. To all my inner circle friends, "family", and coaches, who believed, endorsed, and encouraged me; you are a true treasure in my heart, thank you.

- **Dawna Campbell**

FOREWORD

You're wrong if you think this book is about budgets, savings, mutual funds, bonds, insurance, and real estate. Although these things are good, there is something better.

Those topics are the right answer to the wrong question. Sure, I can teach you about any of those topics, but the better questions aren't about investment tools and wealth strategies. Rather, the best questions are about the mindset and the heartset that can attract prosperity when mastered through an experienced mentor.

Your real journey begins when you not only ask the right questions, but when you start to study the intuitive decision makeover with quantifiable results.

This is Dawna's life's work and what she's dedicated her life to. The books and documentaries on physics and mathematics that most of us would use to help us fall asleep is something she absorbs like a sponge for fun.

You will learn a lot from this book, because it's not just the metaphysical and intuitive geniuses, rather, it is also the scientific and the proven practices of the prosperous.

You can solve some of the greatest mysteries of the Universe through this book, and the reward of abundance is nothing short of a miracle for many.

I challenge you to suspend disbelief, consider the teachings and divine truths revealed in these pages, and to experiment for yourself what Dawna has already proven to be true in her own life. That you can attract abundance in proven and predictable ways. That math and magic do coexist. That physics and financial fitness are tied together.

Dawna will show you how to both play and practice a life of learning, lifestyle, and legacy. It takes a healthy relationship with your intuition and massive amounts of consistent action, but the true freedom is priceless.

The future of financial fitness will continue to look different, and this book is just another bold step in that direction.

You are being given the chance to choose abundance through this book. Take it. - **David Fagan**

David T. Fagan is the former CEO of Guerrilla Marketing, which sold over 23 million books in 62 languages all over the world, as well as the former owner of LCO Communications, a Beverly Hills PR firm that has represented 58 Academy Award Winners, 34 Grammy Winners, and 43 *New York Times* Best Sellers.

He has been featured on *Fox & Friends, the Today Show, The Washington Post, Forbes, Investor's Business Daily, Your World with Neil Cavuto,* Fox's *The Five,* and *What's Happening Now,* to name a few. He's won major awards for publishing, publicity, and even the Entrepreneur Educator of the Year Award from Inc 500 Infusionsoft.

David is the best-selling author of several books, including *Word Genius: What to Say and How to Say It, Guerrilla Parenting: How to Raise an Entrepreneur, Cracking the Icon Code: How to Become an Icon in Your Industry Through Your Advice, Image and Expertise,* and *From Invisible to Invincible: How to Make Your Presence Felt.* He's an international speaker in places as far away as Dubai, Bangladesh, Kenya, and Australia. He has shared the stage with everyone from Former Secretary of Defense Dr. Bob Gates to Mark Victor Hansen.

David is the father of eight children (four girls and four boys), and even has one grandchild. He is married to Isabel Donadio, and they live in the Phoenix, Arizona area.

You have been lied to for so long. I actually heard the same lies and know that most of the people who share them don't really know any better. You must have also heard some truth somewhere along the way, but with so many competing thoughts and ideas, it can be hard to tell which ones to really take to heart.

This Matters Most

You can become a truth-seeker and truth-teller like me, but first you have to really understand what I mean when I say "financially fit". After all, it may not be for you.

When we hear the words "financially fit", there is an initial impression of how to invest, eliminate debt, and create a world of wealth. If this is your impression, you might be disappointed. I am going to share these things with you, but with a twist and from a nontraditional viewpoint. I want to go deeper, below the surface of releasing debt and adding to your investments.

There are many financial gurus today who have written and spoken about finance and money. There are several hundred, maybe even thousands of books of on being financially fit in the business and money categories. When I was in the financial industry, I owned and read many of these books. Many of them are considered "the greats" that redefined the financial industry of today.

Redefining Financial Fitness

You need a new financial vocabulary, and I am going to give it to you. This ever-evolving world requires an upgrade.

Over the last 25 years of my professional career, I have discovered the problem. The books, speakers, and authors come from a perspective of the conscious mind. Some may address the mindset that is needed, but even that is from a conscious viewpoint, implying if we do these things, money will come. As far as I am aware, there has not been a book that dove deeper into the subconscious to align us with the energy of money until this one.

When we have released outdated patterns and programs that do not work in our new environment and align with the energy of money, we can become instant manifesters. We are more powerful than we think when it comes to money creation.

Financially Fit is for the person who wants to be fit in their mind financially first, and then use all the tools given to us by our favorite financial guru. This book is all the tools I wish I had before my financial career.

Einstein's Brain

Our consciousness accounts for 10 percent of our awareness, and this is how the financial world is approached. There was a study that measured Albert Einstein's brain, and his consciousness level was 10 percent. Well, I will be the first to admit that I am not Einstein, but I do like whole, round numbers. This begs the question, what is the other 90 percent of our brain doing?

When we look under the mask the consciousness, what is underneath is subconscious, the remaining 90 percent. The subconscious records all of the events and experiences that we have in life, assigning emotions and feelings to those events, creating an automatic pattern for us to live by. The subconscious is incredibly powerful and can override any of our conscious awareness and thinking –and most of the time – we are unaware of this happening!

The Big Disconnect

We rely on what we consciously know, without understanding the why of the subconscious. Simon Sinek said it best when he coined the phrase, "What's your why". *Financially Fit* is about understanding the internal why from your subconscious.

Robbed at Nine

One of my clients came to me to understand why he had a pattern of failure. He owned several high-end companies. Two of them were doing okay and staying profitable. The third company kept going further into debt. He also wanted more joy in his – and watching a company he built from the ground up start to dissolve was not his idea of joy. Together, we uncovered an experience in his early childhood that was preventing his financial success.

He was nine years old and was very excited—exuberant really—about the gift his father was purchasing for him. When they went to the counter to make payment on the purchase, the credit card was declined. Standing there disappointed, he did not understand what had just happened. Nothing was explained. He only knew that he was robbed of his joy and was not going home with his gift.

This experience created a subconscious pattern that impacted his everyday life. Using some of the processes in *Financially Fit*, we were able to see the correlation and change the subconscious pattern to create the reality of a world of wealth. He understood that he was looking externally to find fulfillment of happiness, like many of us do. When this pattern changed, he had "aha" moments of inspiration that were life-changing for him.

From Mindset to Lifestyle

Financially Fit is not only an internal mindset, but a lifestyle and a way to live. When the subconscious is in alignment with what we consciously know, we become unstoppable and unlimited.

Throughout this book, I am going to show you how to access parts of the subconscious that created patterns in your life. I am also going to share with you how our words that are used to describe the feelings we have correlate to the financial world, and what to do to start changing them. There are topics such as how money relates to sex, as well as how money debts create energy deficits within the subconscious.

Some of these topics you may not agree with. There may not consciously be an understanding of the correlations with the topic and how it relates to money. Sometimes, you might feel triggered. That is okay. The trigger is an indication that there is something in the subconscious that is not in alignment with what you consciously know and an area that can be improved upon.

I have also included some meditations that I have written for you. No, I don't have the expectation that you are going to sit around all day "aum-ing" in a lotus position. Meditation is a doorway to accessing the subconscious. Science and physics have shown that when certain brain waves are accessed, such as alpha and theta, we can enter the subconscious mind. For the purpose of Financially Fit, you only have to read the meditation that is offered, preferably out loud, and it will start to work on the subconscious mind.

You might ask, "Why are these things important?" When the subconscious and the conscious are in pure alignment, only then can we access a world of living an authentic life of abundance and prosperity. This is what it means to be truly financially fit.

Regardless of your profession, I challenge you to dive in, access your own subconscious, and create a world of abundance and prosperity for yourself.

CHAPTER 1

Abundance for All

You deserve an abundant life of happiness, prosperity, and love. You might think that I don't even know you, so I can't say that with any level of certainty, but know that simply because you are reading this book.

This means you wanted, you listened, you took action, and you are following through. The Universe opens up to people like you. I know this because I took similar steps that I'm sharing with you in these pages.

My Discovery Decades

Over the last 25 years, I have been exploring the topic of creating an abundant life. The first ten years I was licensed to sell securities as a financial planner, chartered mutual fund counselor, and managing principal, helping middle class America get ahead with money and cash flow while protecting their investments. I believed so strongly that everyone deserved a life of abundance and well-being, I dedicated my life to helping others achieve these same goals.

During that time, I hired and trained other advisors and was responsible for $500 million dollars of *other people's money*. This was an incredibly stressful career, combined with worry and fear. If the funds didn't perform, the clients didn't make a profit, and they were upset. Although there were so many external factors beyond anyone's control, like the stock market and mutual fund picks by the portfolio managers, the responsibility fell on the advisor's shoulders. The financial planners would take into consideration the client's goals and what they desired to achieve with their money objectives. However, how the client felt about the success or failure of their goals was not explored, and the clients had just as much stress and worry as everyone else.

Hospital Time

The additional stress and worry added to the decline of my health. After a period of time, I was unable to digest food and had been in and out of the hospital. This spilled over into my personal life and relationships that I was unable to emotionally digest. My marriage of 14 years dissolved, creating an extra strain on the finances and eventually became financially devastated, filing bankruptcy as a single parent with children.

I had followed all the rules that were taught about money, yet the abundance stream was cut off. As my career was ending in financial services, I moved to an ashram (spiritual living community) to study healing and meditation with masters. During this time, I was secretly living in complete fear for my life. The spiritual partner I was with became physically abusive, isolating me from society and attempting to separate me from my children.

I made a decision to live fully and knew that I had to discover a different way. This decision truly ignited my path to be a healer and experience the good things in life. The next decade was dedicated to researching, learning about subconscious brain patterns, brain waves, and how the energy body worked with our divine essence that we call a spirit or soul. I became certified in several healing methods that took you inside to find your answers, took training courses, studied many meditation techniques, and learned as much as I could about natural medicine, nutrition, herbs, and supplements.

How it All Started

During the last two years working in the financial industry, I had been severely sick. I had been working long hours with a toddler and newborn baby, and the responsibility for other people's money was quite stressful. My husband at the time was out of work and chose to return to school to become a pilot. Debt increased, student loans were mounting, and the burden all fell on me. My body was breaking down, and eventually, I was in extreme pain. I desired better health, so I went on a diet, counted calories, kept a food log, went to the gym, had a personal trainer, and still kept gaining weight. The next year, I changed gyms and trainers, and nothing worked.

My Body Wasn't Right

The office building replaced the carpet, and without proper ventilation, the smell of the chemical glue was strong and toxic. During a lunch break, I stopped by a takeout drive-through to purchase a salad for healthy eating. While eating the salad, I was preparing for a corporate trainer who was arriving from New York the next day. The next morning, I was in so much pain I could barely move. Somehow, I got the children off to their destinations. When I returned home, the salad I ate the day before did not digest, and that was the first trip to the doctor.

My healthcare provider sent me to the emergency room for further testing. Being admitted overnight, the next day, I was sent home with a stomach viral infection. I was informed there wasn't anything that could be, since it was a virus, and if I got worse, "please come back". A few days later, I returned with acute pancreatitis. I recall thinking that I would never wish this on another person, and that childbirth was easier than to experience this pain. I really thought I was going to die.

Still Hurting

I returned to the hospital every couple of days, spending 30 out of 45 days there. During this time, my office work was brought to me daily. If I didn't at least sign the investment recommendations checking for compliance with securities, none of the advisors or I got paid. The healthcare providers were unable to determine why I had been sick without an apparent cause. I knew if I ate, everything hurt, and if I didn't eat, everything hurt.

Over the next two years, I maxed out my health insurance, exhausting every possible lead as to why I was in such a condition. I had been to my family medicine doctor, gastroenterologists, specialists, and doctors who utilized internal medicine. Test after test, there were not any answers.

My medication was changed every two weeks, and with every "please come back" trip, I started to develop allergic reactions to the medications prescribed to me. My body was on toxic overload.

Eventually, my body failed the gallbladder function test and based on the test results, the decision was made to remove it. The gallbladder was sent in for testing after it was removed, showing healthy, perfect tissue, without stones or a sign of cancer. I was left dumbfounded. I was told that if the symptoms that I was experiencing did not improve after recovery, to "please come back". A year later, the pain became more severe, and I did not "please come back".

What Did I miss?

I asked this question to myself often. After doing my own research with natural medicine, I chose to allow my body to detoxify. With a fresh perspective, I sought out an energy healer who used Chinese medicine and was a naturopath doctor.

During my intake, I was asked several questions that I had never been asked before. Questions about my home life, work life, and my daily routine. I was treated with a form of energy work and sent home. I returned for the same treatment every couple of weeks, and one day, I realized my stomach had stopped hurting. This was also the time I realized that I was unable to emotionally digest the energy of anger in the marriage. Slowly, I realized that my relationship was not in alignment with my morals, values, and virtues of who I was as my authentic being.

The stomach area is about digesting life. When this is not possible, energetically, you are not able to digest life. Emotionally, I was not able to digest life around me, and this showed in my physical body as being unable to digest food. I physically created this in my body, ignoring life and ignoring the signs that were being offered.

Thought Form Energy Healing

Our beliefs are composed of our thought patterns, which are fueled from the feelings we choose to feel. These patterns of behavior can be changed instantly by changing the feelings associated with the thought that was created. In every moment of life, every vibration exists and is offered. The feelings that were generated within merely got stuck on one vibration and failed to recognize that other feelings were possible. Every thought that is produced, every word that is spoken, and every feeling programs the subconscious through the mental and emotional body, and eventually enters into the physical body.

It's All About Energy

The body combined with the divine essence creates us as electro-magnetic beings. The body produces energy from the brain through the nervous system, moving up and down. This electrical energy magnetically sends out signals to attract back the feelings that fuel the thoughts through a gravitational force. This is what creates an energy field around the body called an aura, and is measurable through quantum physics.

When a negative energy response is felt, the energy field condenses and decreases, keeping the negative thought form close to the body. Negative thought forms are fueled by low feelings, such as anger, depression, sadness, anxiety, or frustration.

The energy field around the body will shrink until it is absorbed into the physical body. This is how sickness and illness can reside in a body, creating ill health. A positive energy response expands your energy field.

The body's magnetic attraction with high vibrating thought forms fueled by positive feelings. Positive feelings and words, such as love, kindness, peace, gratitude, and happiness keep the energy body strong, increasing the immune system and overall good health.

What is on the inside?

Every thought and feeling takes place on the inside and keeps either a balance or imbalance creating the emotions. When the emotions and feelings are changed on the inside, new thoughts develop, and a new internal balance is the result. When sadness is felt, sadness returns. The same is true with happiness.

Happiness on the inside creates happiness on the outside. The inside world is always creating the outside world—or at least having an extreme effect on it. The outside world is always fluid and changing based on the internal thought forms of everyone, which can alter our internal state of being. Keeping an internal balance is the key to having the energy move from the inside out bringing back the reality that we create.

Business Clients, Personal Issues

Private clients come to my practice wanting to know how to increase the abundance in their life. The process outlined in *Financially Fit* is the same process that I use with clients and on myself. From all of my experiences, I learned that there is a silver lining in all situations. There is even a silver lining in the silver lining, and this is what I call "A Gift". These gifts are designed for us to learn from all the life situations that are offered—the good, the bad, and the ugly. The healing industry taught me that my thoughts created my reality, but the real secret is that there is an energy behind those thoughts that give them fuel. There is a real, raw, powerful energy behind those thoughts that is fueled by how we choose to feel. When we change the fuel behind the thoughts, we change the reality that we are experiencing.

Abundance in the Making

Living a life of abundant thinking, creating happiness, prosperity, and love through better health, increased wealth, and enhanced relationships is the aim of *Financially Fit*. These areas are all interconnected. How we feel about one area in life will reflect in the other areas of our life, physically, emotionally, mentally, and spiritually. When these changes are made, the patterns of behavior shift, changing the beliefs we have, and we take back our power to create a life on purpose.

CHAPTER 2

An Inside Job

The collective conscious energy believes money solves all problems and provides a sense of freedom and happiness. A freedom to be and do what is desired, when it is desired, which, by default, would create happiness.

From the Inside Out

Here is the mistake that is made. Money is external, while happiness and freedom are internal states of being. By believing that money is a problem-solver, the solution is outside of ourselves. This outward view determines the decisions and feelings for the solution. The opposite of this viewpoint is what is the real truth. The solution is always inside, the internal state of being, never outside.

The perception is that if there is plenty of money, there is a freedom to go anywhere and do anything that is desired. Some see this as the truth, but a higher truth is that this freedom is inherent, regardless of the amount of money a person may have. This is all a matter of perspective and feeling. Some people feel completely free and happy with very little money because of less materialism to take care of. Others who have lots of money may feel the worry and stress, restricting the freedom to have happiness.

Everyone wants to feel abundant. This word, abundance, is automatically associated with a thought and feeling of money.

This is a subconscious thought pattern that most are not aware of. To really live abundantly, abundance should be in all areas of our lives, physically, mentally, emotionally, and spiritually. Abundance, prosperity, and wealth are about more than just money. To truly be abundant in our health, wealth, and relationships, those qualities of happiness, prosperity, and love need to be there.

What is at your center?

Imagine a Venn diagram with three overlapping circles that represent what is at the center of our being. The outside larger circles say: health, wealth, and relationships. In the intersecting circle parts, it says happiness, prosperity, and love. What is at the very center?

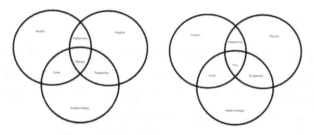

Social conditioning interprets money as the very center of those circles that create happiness, prosperity, and love. Here is a little secret. Money is *not* inside of you. Last time I checked the inside of someone, there were organs, muscles, bones, and tissues, and a divine essence, confidently verified by doctors. Honestly, I have never seen money literally inside of a person. The conclusion is that money didn't create your physical body.

The Big Money Mistake

Money, being outside the body, can be seen, touched, held, and smelled. Money can be exchanged for goods and services and comes in different forms: gold and silver, dollars in different currencies, and digital. Money can also be part of a bartering system, such as a cow for a pig. (Imagine if that was inside of you!) Mistakenly, money is often at the center of our being-ness.

All of the components that are on the inside allow for the physical body to exist. This includes a divine essence that is an energy vibration print that makes up the energy field that goes around the body. The feelings and thoughts that are produced in the brain and body encode this energy field and is the energy vibration that is offered. The thoughts and feelings we have about money is a part of this. The energy that leaves the body is what allows the attraction, or non-attraction, for the financial abundance that is desired in life.

When you think about money, what are the feelings that you experience? Do you feel worry, stress, or fear? Is there happiness, joy, and peace? Do you have some combination of the two sets of emotions? Some people are content with the money supply that they have, but that does not mean that they are automatically happier.

The Prosperity Paradox

People who have an abundance of money may not have happiness, and other people without money may have happiness. There are people who have lots of money that are happy, and others without money with unhappiness. The happiness inside of someone is not dictated by the amount of money and more money does not guarantee happiness.

People with plenty of money may have more materialism, and for a short time, have happiness. This is a temporary feeling, and the search for the next happiness begins. Often, the feeling will dissipate. With this model of money bringing happiness, there is a continued search for looking to the outside world for continued buying of happiness. Everlasting happiness is not available for purchase.

Regardless of the social conditioning, if a person was honest with themselves, there would be a realization that money is not at the center of being-ness. The core of being-ness is a divine essence, the true nature of energy essence, a Universal Force of Love. This is a pure, raw energy that makes everything in the Universe.

In an excerpt from a letter to his daughter, Albert Einstein said:

"There is an extremely powerful force that, so far, science has not found a formal explanation to. It is a force that includes and governs all others, and is even behind any phenomenon operating in the Universe and has not been identified by us. This universal force is LOVE. When scientists looked for a unified theory of the Universe, they forgot the most powerful unseen force. This force explains everything and gives meaning to life."

The divine essence is accessible inside of every person and can be used to create unlimited health, wealth, and relationships. These feeling qualities that are felt and experienced are a part of the divine essence. This essence is what created you and the physical body. This is the Force of Love, an unconditional love energy that created you.

Knowing Inside from Out

There is not a feeling or emotion that is experienced outside of who we are. This entire process takes place inside the body. The thoughts that are thought about is what produces the feelings that offer the vibrational experience that is created. The feelings behind the thoughts that are felt with the money will produce the life experience.

If you have stress and worry when money is thought about, stress and worry will be produced inside. Over time, feelings will break down the physical body and dis-ease will set in. If there is happiness and peace when money is thought about, the physical body will produce these feelings and will build up and have a strong physical body. How thoughts and feelings are generated around money is what is important to understand.

Direct Experience and Money

Feelings about money come from the first direct experiences associated with money. The initial experiences with money usually took place between the ages of four and ten years old, and were taught to us by parents, grandparents, siblings, or teachers. How the philosophy of money was taught influenced the feelings and behaviors on a subconscious level.

As a Kid

Growing up, I was taught to never talk about money. Money was an intimate topic only to be discussed between two committed married people, not to be shared with anyone else. I was not allowed to speak about money or ask for money, and I was certainly not allowed to share. Money was a taboo topic and a secret. My parents were incredibly stressed, worried, and ashamed about money. There was never enough money, and assistance with money was required. Money was an embarrassment, and during my formative years, I absorbed all of the same feelings my parents had around money.

My parents lived strictly in survival mode, creating just enough money to live on. Sometimes, not even enough. Often, state government assistance programs were utilized just to eat. Being observant, I realized that if I needed the basics of life, I was going to have to provide them for myself. This is what started my direct experience with money. After learning that money was stressful, not having enough, that I needed to work hard for it, worry about, and never talking about money, I was already exhausted when I started my first job at age 14.

Sarah the Money Magnet

Every person has a different direct experience with money. Sarah, a client, was able to create and manifest money. She was quite good at money generation from a very young age, a skill she learned from her parents. Her direct experience about money was a little different.

Sarah was never able to hold on to the money. She could create money, but was unable to save money. This was a pattern she learned from her parents. Her parents were always using the extra money that was created to improve their home and various upgrades, such as nicer cars.

Through this experience, Sarah was repeating the same pattern. Money that was created always went to something else, rather than the vacation she wanted. Her experiences created a continuous cycle of always creating money that went to fund things other than what she truly wanted. There was always a feeling that money was always slipping through her fingers.

You Need to Question Yourself

You should start to consider what your childhood was like when it came to money. Look at the feelings and experiences you had around money growing up. Once there is an understanding, a new perspective can be created.

Your feelings that were first created about money are the subconscious programming that creates patterns and automatic responses that are experienced today. If the feelings are a low, heavy feeling form, such as stress, worry, anger, frustration, these need to be released from the subconscious. As an energetic being, these subconscious feelings are the electrical signals being sent out to the world to magnetically attract back to reinforce how you feel.

Rewiring

The new feelings are what the subconscious can be reprogrammed with to have a different experience. The replacement energy is what we want the subconscious to recognize. This is usually a lighter feeling, such as passion, creativity, happiness, balance, or peace. The subconscious is teaching how to receive the higher feeling from the lower. If frustration was the direct experience with money and the higher replacement feeling is peace, then frustration is teaching how to have peace.

A Volunteer in the Audience

Bob was attending a motivational presentation of mine, and he volunteered for an illustration of how this works. My first question for Bob was what he wanted to change in his life. Bob shared that he wanted to create "more" for his family, financially. He had plenty, they were comfortable, but he wanted the "more".

Bob didn't want to be greedy, but wanted to provide a bit more than he had before. I asked him how he currently felt about not "having more", and he said, "frustrated". I asked about his childhood and if he could recall an experience about being frustrated.

When Bob tapped into a feeling of frustration, he recalled at age 11, his parents got divorced. The "having more" was split in half due to the divorce. I asked Bob how he would rather feel by "having more". His answer included pride and to be proud of what he accomplished. Bob was unaware the subconscious was releasing the energy of frustration, which only returned more frustration to him.

Once Bob recognized that he wanted to feel proud, a new sensation came over him. Bob's subconscious is now sending the energy signal of feeling proud to attract "having more", rather than the old feeling of frustration. The past memory at age 11 was recalled, and Bob's perception of the experience shifted from frustration to a sense of pride.

Rewriting History

When reviewing his story again, the experience he remembered was different. The events of the divorce remained, but this time, Bob was not affected. He was happy riding his bike and having more fun. Bob's consciousness did all of the work to reprogram the subconscious.

Once he understood the signal that the subconscious was sending out, he realized what was stopping him from achieving more. Bob's life changed in a moment when the feeling shifted from frustration to pride. Today, Bob is happily producing the "more" he asked for, and the only thing that changed was the energy vibration that he was offering.

You can breakthrough like Sarah and Bob by starting with analyzing your past experiences looking for moments that made an impact on you. You are defined yourself by these decisions that you started making after both good and bad experiences.

You should compare the direct experience feelings and the desired higher feelings. Which set of feelings will help you create more happiness in life? If the higher desired feelings are more powerful and positive than the direct experience feelings, revisit those childhood experiences from the higher feelings and experience the event from this new mindset.

CHAPTER 3

Money Mind Imprints

Money beliefs also come from the DNA that we are born with. DNA is the instructions that are encoded in the cells that give a blueprint or operating instructional manual. The DNA is encoded with lots of feelings and beliefs from the generations before giving instructions on how to interact with money. What was learned from the past is handed down.

This is the study of epigenetics. The generations before me worked hard, long hours for money. These feelings created beliefs passed down through DNA, giving an instruction code that if I want money, I have to work long, hard hours. My DNA instruction book said that was true, and the subconscious took over recreating the pattern of me working long hard hours for money.

Encoded Inside

Bill was a farmer whose main objective was clearing his issues around money. He had been through a divorce a few years back and lost everything, but managed to keep the farm. In looking at the subconscious patterns in the DNA, it was discovered that in Bill's lineage, every other generation had an event where they lost everything, but managed to keep the farm. This was encoded in Bill's DNA operating manual. His DNA executed these operating instructions and repeated a genetic pattern.

Feelings around money can also be programmed through the genetic DNA heritage and can create conflict in the subconscious. Part of my DNA heritage includes Native American and European ancestry. The Natives lived off the land, used everything they had, and did not have use for "white man's" money. There was a common exchange of goods, and the focus was on the entire benefit of the tribe. This was in direct conflict with my European ancestry that used money as an exchange system, purchasing the goods and services for the individual family unit.

Social Conditioning and Money

Feelings and beliefs about money can also be programmed into the subconscious through social conditioning and the media. This includes the events that happened in the history of the land. A great example is the United States Stock Market Crash of 1929. After becoming an independent nation from Great Britain, a new money supply was established. The stock market had been created for trading, and in 1929, everything collapsed. People became jobless, the money supply diminished, and poverty set in. This triggered the Great Depression in the 1930s, which prompted the media to come out with headlines "A Nation Crippled". A physical crippling took place, and polio was the result. Franklin Delano Roosevelt, who had polio, was elected as the next President, and brought the nation out of crippling to re-establish financial stability. With social conditioning, those who resonated with the fear of financial devastation that the media shared resonated with the energy of polio.

Spiritual Essence and Money

Through the spiritual essence, the subconscious can be programmed with feelings and beliefs about money. The subconscious never rests and is always learning. These are lessons that are learned from other lifetimes or from dreams. The subconscious creates oaths and vows on a spiritual level to experience, such as a vow of poverty, a vow of silence, a vow of suffering, or a vow of sacrifice. The subconscious creates these vows for the spiritual growth of our divine essence. The vows imply limitation, restriction, and conditions. This is simply not true. The divine essence is unlimited abundance, expansive and unlimited.

Divine essence is the true identity of your soul energy print. Instead of making vows, offer a higher feeling of blessings with money. The blessing of financial freedom, the blessing of abundance, the blessing of prosperity, or the blessing of security will align with your divine essence and offer greater returns.

Money Secrets

Money is designed to be fluid and simply an energy exchange system for the goods and services purchased. This doesn't mean that all the money is spent when it is earned, nor that all the money is held onto that is generated. Having in-flows and out-flows are natural. When income is earned, money is released into the world, paying expenditures, and this opens the door for more to return. This is the *first secret* of creating abundance: allowing money to be fluid in life.

How you feel about money is the *second secret*. Money doesn't create happiness, but happiness does return money. Heavier feelings are blocks to returning abundance and are not in alignment with the divine essence. Heavy feelings keep the body stressed, creating dis-ease such as adrenal fatigue, restless sleep, or anxiety/depression cycles. This changes quickly when the focus shifts to true happiness to allow abundance and prosperity to flow.

The *third secret* is kindness. When a person is internally happy, there is a natural connection with kindness. Being kind with time and money in service to others can create many opportunities. People will naturally want to share in goodwill simply because the energy being offered is magnetic. Opportunities will be offered, and people will want to work with you.

As money increases, respond back with money. Generosity is the *fourth secret*. Money can be used for personal benefit and the benefit of others. Be a philanthropist, fund projects, or start a foundation for the betterment of humanity. Giving back creates an endless cycle of receiving, and you are divinely supported with all that is created.

Money and Passion

Most people are doing what is needed to earn a paycheck and not what they are passionate about. There are several fears around sharing what you are passionate about. The first fear is that money will not return. This subconscious fear program is keeping a sense of feeling "safe" from going broke. Another fear is being unaccepted by others, so you don't share your passions, or on the flip side, a fear of having your passions accepted and being overwhelmed with abundance. These fears take hold when money is placed at the center, rather than the divine essence. If the passion energy flows out of the divine essence instead, this is what is returned, and money follows.

Money and Freedom

Social conditioning believes money provides freedom. What money provides is a temporary happiness that produces a false sense of freedom. The temporary happiness changes to boredom, and a cycle of creating the next happiness begins. This doesn't result in long-term happiness or freedom, keeping us a prisoner in the system. Freedom of happiness is there, regardless of the money. Money doesn't decide how to, where to, and who to spend time with. That is an internal decision based on what will create happiness.

The Medicine Woman

Some of my studies included working with a Medicine Woman on an Indian reservation. She knew that I had concern and worry with money being single, jobless, with two small children to take care of. The wisdom she imparted with me is still strong in my mind.

"On one hand, money provides a sense of freedom that allows you to pay bills, debts, and do things desired, but what would you really do if you had infinite money? You think you would have more freedom with more money, but freedom is a mindset. There is a balance between money, passion, and freedom that must be obtained."

Often, I contemplated her words. I did have freedom of time. My thoughts were not being consumed with outside influences allowing me to be present in the moment. I did wonder how some of the bills would be paid.

Trust was a new discovery that money would always be there when it was needed. The greatest lesson that was learned was that money did not affect the essence of who I am, and that provided the greatest freedom. There is a delicate balance between money and the divine essence of a person's being.

CHAPTER 4

Are you Happy?

A previous employer asked everyone on a routine basis "Are you happy?" The question was so frequent when she entered the room, automatically you started assessing the level of happiness. Many scales for the internal happiness meter were used for measurement when I was approached with this question.

Sometimes, I would say "yes", but that brought more questions, such as "Are you truly sure?" Other times, I said, "Well, I am mostly happy," or "Today, I am happy, but yesterday I was not." A favorite response was quantifying happiness such as, "I am 85 percent happy", as if happiness could be measured in this way. Avoiding answering this question was not a good choice either. There wasn't an escape, except to deal with my mindset.

The Glass is Half...Something

Mental notes were taken daily on internal happiness. I quickly realized that the focus was mostly directed on the things that brought unhappiness. Although a natural tendency to focus on what is lacking, subconsciously, I was creating more *unhappiness* and unwanted experiences. Being programmed through life experiences, social conditioning, and the media, my destiny seemed to have an outcome of unhappiness.

Happiness is an Inside Job

Successful people living an abundant and affluent life have the same question as everyone, "How can I be happy?" They are uncertain how to answer, because money was a distraction keeping them in a state of doing, rather than being.

One way to discover internal happiness is by keeping a happiness journal. Keep a journal where all the things that brought happiness are recorded. This is a little different than a gratitude journal. Happy moments are recorded, rather than thankful moments. This process allows a discovery of the divine essence. Record the happy moments of when opportunities of happiness could be shared. What brings each person happiness is different and a personal journey. This self-discovery process is what allows the divine essence to sing full of joy. When thoughts and feelings are focused on the energy of happiness, you feed yourself happiness. Happiness feeds happiness.

When true happiness happens, a chemical reaction occurs in the brain releasing "feel good" hormones. This is the first way to becoming financially fit. When happiness is recognized, you become it. Fill up with happiness, and the outside world will shift and respond to the happiness, bringing more.

Reflect back at the end of the day and remember the happy moments that were experienced, and write them in the journal. A simple list is all that is needed:

* Received a letter in the mail from son in the Army.

* Sharing a smile with the store clerk.

* A client received abundance in their life.

* Spring is here, and the flowers are blooming.

* Out in nature for a hike.

You can also take the higher feelings and start the happiness journal from that mindset. Write down the higher feelings and how those feelings help to produce happiness. A different way of recording a happiness journal is to use video or voice recorders, if writing is not the preferred method.

CHAPTER 5

Your Worth or Net Worth?

Words are a combination of our energetic thoughts, feelings, and emotions. Regardless, if the words are spoken out loud, the thoughts, feelings, and emotions send energy signals through our auric field or energy body. These electrical impulses move from the brain through the nervous system and send out a signal, or wave pattern, to the world. These waves magnetically draw back the thoughts, feelings, and emotions that were originally sent out to create experiences.

Chain Reaction

If you think or feel poor, the brain will create a chemical response going through the nervous system that enters the energy field around you to attract back the feeling of being poor. In this example, the frequency of feeling poor is being sent through the energy field to return. If you think or feel rich, the brain will also send the chemical messengers through the nervous system, out the energy field to return the feeling of being rich.

Emotional Awareness

People are aware of about 10 percent of the thoughts and emotions that are sending out this energetic information. The remaining 90 percent resides in the subconscious, and these energy signals are also released through the energy body undetected. The subconscious records all the information since conception and records everything.

As life is experienced, the brain will start assigning the feelings that were felt during the experiences. The only difference between the conscious and subconscious is level of awareness. The subconscious is an automatic operating system that triggers responses to life events. Just like breathing, the process happens without awareness.

Creature of Every Kind

Every living being has an energetic vibrational frequency that can be measured and felt. Imagine walking down the hallway to the weekly sales meeting. The knowingness of the type of meeting can be felt beforehand from the energy of the room. The vibrational energy patterns of the people in the meeting are emitting a frequency. Instinctually, this is how we know when we pass by someone if they are a pleasant or dangerous person. Each person emits their own frequency and has the ability to intuitively "read" this energy to make decisions.

The frequencies in the energy field produced by feelings are emitting to the world and everyone around. This creates the world that is experienced from the outside.

Awareness of the feelings and the thoughts that are held is important. How you feel about money, food, health, and relationships leaves the energy field to magnetically attract back the vibrational match to you.

Energy Doesn't Lie

Words, whether thought or spoken, are sent out to the Universe, the context of the words is not taken into consideration. Words are part of the 10 percent conscious awareness that is produced. The Universe reads 100 percent of all the energy signals all the time, the conscious and the subconscious combined. As the signals are sent out, the vibrational match will return, producing the results of the signals.

Imagine a radio tower or satellite. The radio tower sends out an energy transmission for sound frequency for a song to play. This is a transmitter. The radio is a receiver and when dialed to a certain station, will pick up the song being transmitted.

You're Like a Two-Way Radio

The result is being able to listen to the song being broadcast. People are both transmitters and receivers. When a thought is produced, the signal sends out as a transmission. Others can receive that transmission and transmit back the same thought that was produced. Just like the radio station, the people who pick up and resonate with the thought will broadcast it back.

The feelings that are produced behind the thought gives the thought fuel. If a feeling/thought transmission is strong enough before calling a friend, that friend might say, "I was just thinking about you." That friend received the transmission beforehand.

Everyone is constantly sending and receiving thought signals fueled by feelings.

Decided to Start Dating

Sue had decided to start dating again, desiring a relationship. She sent out the energy signals and immediately met someone. Over the next several months, Sue realized what she wanted to experience and what he wanted to experience were completely opposite.

Sue wanted someone she could talk to, have a conversation with, and feel heard. He only wanted to have a good time, party, and watch TV. Sue and her partner were a vibrational match in the beginning with a love for adventure, but as the relationship developed, old routines set in, and the relationship started to stagnate. Sure, it was fun and new at first, but as the relationship continued, it lost its luster.

The relationship balance became disrupted and resistance from Sue started to develop, pushing her partner away. Sue didn't want to be around him anymore. Her resistance energy vibration kept pushing him away and grew so strong that they parted their own separate ways, without having closure.

Regardless of the context of the energy that the energy was created in, the Universe reads 100 percent of the energy vibration. Sue was only resisting the energy of the person she was dating, but the Universe only read "resistance". Sue encountered resistance in every area of her life, not just in resisting the partner. Sue was met with resistance in every area of her life. Her happiness, friendship, income – everything was resisted energetically. The Universe was matching Sue's vibrational pattern, giving her back what she was sending out. Sue was unaware of the signal that she was sending out from the subconscious.

This is how experiences are created from the inside out. Through feelings and emotions, thoughts are out into words with emotion. The Universe reads the emotional energy frequency and sends the frequency back to you. Just like the radio transmitter and receiver, there is not a distinction between the topics. The Universe is only responding to the feelings being produced about the topics.

A Double-Edged Sword

The words used to describe the financial system are the exact same words that are used to describe our divine essence. The words are identical. The feelings implied when using the words are also identical. Remember, there is not a distinction between the words, only an energetic reading of the energy behind the words.

The words that are spoken come from inside of us. Each word that you use has a vibration frequency fueled by feelings, regardless of if the words are describing ourself or our financial position.

The Universe Acts

There is not a difference between using words that describe your divine essence and the words that describe money. When feelings and emotions are applied to your words, the Universe responds back. The Universe does not respond to the situation of how the words are being used, only the feeling frequency behind the words.

You Divine Essence	Your Money
I want to feel.....	What is my....
Worthy	Net-worth
Appreciated	Appreciation
Valued	Value
Enough	(Do I have) enough
Important	Importance
Matter	Matter
Secure	Financial security
Rich in spirit	Rich in finances
Inside life force energy	Outside life force energy

The words are identical in both columns. How you feel about who you are as a person is programmed in the subconscious.

When the vibrations leave the energy field, the same vibration return back. There is not a distinction to the Universe between how you feel about you and how you feel about money, since the word are the same.

What's at Your Center ?

This is where confusion is created. If money is at the center of happiness, prosperity, and love, the patterns that were created from life experiences will keep repeating. If divine essence is at the center, you can influence money by changing the subconscious programming and sending a different energy through the field.

Can subconscious programs be changed about money? Yes. However when you reach the heart of the matter, it always returns to the divine essence.

The Thought Behind the Thought

When the feelings and emotions are reached deep in the subconscious, they can surface to conscious awareness. Once the consciousness has this awareness, change can be created. This is the first step: to be consciously aware of the thought. By asking questions, we can find the thought behind the thought, behind the thought, back to the originating thought that started the process. The originating thought is a feeling that started the whole chain reaction. This feeling is a pattern that is used to create life experiences every moment of every day. The originating thought always comes back to what a person desired on a soul level.

Every client I have worked with all came to similar conclusions. People want to feel worthy, know that they are enough, that they are loved, and appreciated, they are valued, they are important, and that they matter on a deep soul level. These are incredibly important qualities. On a soul level, the qualities are not fully embraced if the words that are used are associated with different feelings. The vibrational energy has to match.

Unable to feel	If you feel
Worthy	Unworthy to have increased income
Valued	Worried about the value of your portfolio
Appreciated	Stressed about your assets appreciating
Enough	Not enough money in the bank

This sends out mixed frequencies as a transmitter, and the Universe receives mixed up messages. When this happens, there is a delay in the Universe responding, creating a waiting period. Eventually, the Universe will respond back with the stronger frequency that was sent out and return that one. The stronger frequency is often the feelings that are not in alignment with the divine essence. The vibrational feelings of the words with the divine essence need to match the feelings that are used to create money.

When the essence is rich with life, richness in money and finances are returned.

When the essence feels that it is worthy, net worth will increase.

When the essence feels appreciated and valued, money will appreciate in value.

When the essence knows that it is enough, there is enough money.

When the essence feels secure, money returns as a form of security.

The Trick

There is not a decision that needs to be made between essence and money. Both can be achieved at the same time. What is felt on the inside with the essence is created and manifested in the outside world, which includes money. The first part of the "trick" is to have the feeling of feeling rich, and riches will return in the form that is asked for. "I am" statements are powerful and can be repeated to strengthen the conscious awareness, that 10 percent. Wouldn't it be better to strengthen the subconscious energy, since it accounts for 90 percent of the energy, leaving the body to create our life? What if these "I am" statements were programmed into the subconscious and ran on autopilot?

I am worthy.	I am secure.
I am rich.	I am enough.
I am important.	I matter.
I am appreciated.	I am valued.
I am abundant.	I am prosperous.

Every time something good happens, I generate a feeling of abundance and awe in every part of my body. Part of this is the happiness that I feel and can be expressed outwardly. I feel as if I truly won the lottery. This is a subconscious mindset that when programmed in, every day there is an aspect that magnetically brings this feeling of winning the lottery to me. Some days, the wins are smaller. Other days, they are bigger. Regardless, the feeling of always winning the lottery is there. It is automatic, without conscious thought, programmed in my subconscious.

Every time there is a shift and change in our essence, all the other areas of life shift and change. How we think about ourselves creates our health, wealth, and relationships. Here is the second part of the "trick". Once this change is made in the subconscious and the new energy is sent out, the opposite outside world influences of stress, worry, frustration, or fear, are not allowed back in. This is a one-way energy street. This is why it is so incredibly important to understand what is being sent out from the subconscious mind.

CHAPTER 6

Emotionally Attached

Our essence forms emotional connections with the people that are the closest to us. The first connections that are formed are with parents, grandparents, or other people who assisted in upbringing.

These people were the first teachers who taught about the connections with money. Through the emotional connection of the relationships in early childhood, the same bond formed with money.

Your Family

If the family unit was only able to provide the basic necessities in life, food, clothing, shelter, the family unit operated in survival mode. This formed the first emotional connection with money and feelings of "I have to survive" became a part of the divine essence. Survival became the foundation. How the family responded to survival needs taught the connection to how survival needs are responded today as an adult. As the different generation grew, the focus shifted from the survival and physical needs to having emotional needs met.

If your family unit had plenty of money to live, survival was a part of everyday life and not a struggle. Here, the emotional connection with money is different. How the family felt about money, made decisions about using money, and how they interacted with money all had great influence in understanding the emotional connection today with money.

The Money Masks

Was money used to purchase items to feel accepted and loved for themself or purchased to offer acceptance and love to others? Was money spent to overcome guilt from not spending quality time with others? Was purchases made to fill a personal void of feelings that were missing?

These types of emotional connections are not part of the true divine essence. Money used and experienced in this manner fractured the essence and a pattern of looking outside to fill something inside began. The true essence is unlimited expansive energy vibration of divine love. These false connections come into the essence masking the authentic self.

It is very natural to seek emotional connections with others to feel validated, accepted, and confirmed of who we are in life. The imbalance happens when this is sought through other people's opinions or through money to define who and what we are. Money replaced the emotional connection with our essence.

Your Worth or Net Worth?

When I was growing up, 25 cents went a long way and a dollar went even further. $20 was like gold growing up. Today, that same $20 may not even pay for lunch in some places.

The connection with money became the center of the core rather than divine essence. The collective conscious has everybody paying attention to outward things rather than inward. This was taught from our direct experiences, our parents, and collective conscious beliefs. The focus needs to shift back to the internal worth of being-ness. The focus today has shifted from our worth as a divine being to net worth, how much money there is in the account, what the profession of choice is which would all dictate the worth we feel.

This connection with money became the center of our core being-ness rather than our divine essence. The world had us looking outwardly to other things, that money could buy, rather than on the inside of who we are. These came from our direct experiences, our parents, and our group conscious beliefs as a collective. Our focus shifted from our worth as a divine being to our net worth, how much money we had, what we did for a living that would dictate how much money we had, for example. The focus needs to shift back to our own worth.

Net worth does not replace the worth of your divine essence. The soul was created from many infinite possibilities. Out of all the possibilities, the universal force of love energy created you. By pure default, worthiness is given, because you are here. The connection with the Universal Force of Love is the divine essence. Here is an amazing perspective:

"I love this question [Your worth or net worth?]. My husband and I have children in their 20's and we talk about the quality of life, financial choices, and social conditioning with them. My husband and I talk about our different upbringing related to money and share those stories with our kids to clear old family fears. Now, we are focused on releasing all the fearful conditioning about old age and retirement in order to free ourselves to create a flexible, fun, and abundant path for our future. My wish is to always be in my divine clarity so I can understand if the financial books or advice is of the highest service to me. I wish to be free from fear so I always understand when to save, when to spend, when to borrow, and when to share. My financial

worth is in my ability to loving and wisely allow money to flow in and out of my life in perfect divine timing. – Elizabeth"

When the past conditioning of money at the core center of choices is released, the quality of life that is desired can come in through the divine essence. Decision-making comes from a different point of view. The decisions come from the essence rather than the position of money. When decisions are made from the divine essence, a life of happiness, prosperity, and love will be the creation.

Creating Lack

An energy deficit with the divine essence is created when money is at the center of your being-ness lowering a sense of personal worth. Fear often creeps in and lack beliefs will start to surface because the decision making process was based on money rather than the divine essence. Awareness helps if any of these lack beliefs surface through words, thoughts or feelings. This will tell what is at the center of being-ness.

Some thoughts and words are:

* I don't have enough money
* That is expensive
* I can't afford this
* That certainly isn't cheap
* My savings account is draining

When these words are thought or spoken, lack is being affirmed diminishing personal worth.

Social conditioning and history plays a significant role in creating energy deficits and lack mentality. Inflation plays a significant role in defining a sense of personal worth and stealing abundance. Inflation is a concept that money diminishes in value. In 1900, $1 was worth $1. Today, that is about .01 cent due to inflation. Money is not worth as much as it was once before. The dollar is continuously decreasing in value and it certainly does not purchase as much as it did 100 years ago. Subconsciously, money is saying to the divine essence "You are not worth as much as you once were" if money is at the center. This is one of the ways a lack mentally can be created by having the wrong center.

There is less spending power with inflation. An average house in 1959 was about $12,000. Wages in 1959 were also about $12,000, which is a 1:1 ratio. Today, the same average house is about $300,000 but the annual wages are about $60,000. The house is now 5x greater than the earning power. For a bigger picture, in 1959 that income supported two parents, usually only one of them worked, 5 children, a grandparent, and some pets. What was abundant in 1959 is poverty in the world economy today.

A personal sense of worth is greatly diminished if net worth is allowed to define the essence. Abundance shifted to poverty when money is allowed to define the essence. Remember, inflation is an external factor, outside of the divine essence. By keeping a strong sense of personal worth internally, the external factors will not have the same impact.

Creating Real Worth

The good news is that lack can be reversed. Energy does flow both directions. Having a strong sense of self with a sense of purpose and personal worth will influence the environment. How you feel about yourself will change and influence the world. When the personal sense of worth increases your net worth will also increase. This is a direct correlation to how feelings create the experiences in life.

One simple action that can make a large impact is to change the words that are used. If the lack statements are rephrased positively, new feelings of plenty, abundance, and prosperity can be produced, increasing personal worth.

* I have more than enough money
* I have plenty of money
* I am worth it
* My portfolio is always increasing
* My savings account grows everyday

Thinking and Solidifying

When you have a positive thought form combined with the feeling, the personal sense of worth keeps building. With time and repetition, the energy deficit will change to an energy surplus.

Your positive thought forms will generate feelings and build up the sense of personal worth. The subconscious signal changes from the energy body will return that surplus to you, every time.

You should consider some of the common lack phrases that you think or feel that could be creating an energy deficit in your life.

You can them take each one of those phrases and rewrite them in a positive way to create a surplus of abundance, prosperity, and plenty. It's these kinds of actions, activities and processes that rewire your brain for financial fitness.

CHAPTER 7

Essence is Love

What is at the center of divine essence is being worthy of love. Using Albert Einstein's definition, love is the force of energy before it becomes anything in the physical world. When the energy of the essence comes into alignment with personal worth, the ability to create unlimited abundance in life becomes expansive. Here is a daily meditation that can be read to assist in allowing the divine essence to remain in the center.

I Am Worthy of Love

I am worthy, and the Creator will always love me. Through that source energy, the Creator will bring to me people who are capable of loving me as I am of loving them.

I don't have to be or do anything different, but allow and accept the Creator loving me simply because I exist. Through that existence, it is my divine right to be worthy without fear.

Worthy of abundance, love, happiness, prosperity – all that life has to offer. I take off the castings of the world, and know that I am truly worthy of all that life has to offer on this planet.

I step into my divine power as the extension of the Creator, capable of all things, unleashed, unlimited, allowing my divinity to flow. I am worthy of love.

Divine Truth

Your Worth or Net Worth, what are you truly worthy of?

"Both! Create it now!" – *Jennifer*

When your personal worth increases, so does net worth. This is another way to become financially fit. When the emotional energy charge of lack can be shifted to a positive feeling, abundance and prosperity can instantly attract back to us to create it now!

Self-Sabotage with After Thoughts

Manifesting, creating, asking, sometimes begging for the Universe to bring back the very requests sent out, and yet, nothing materializes. Thoughts and feelings of unworthiness, not being listened to or heard, important, or valued start to seep in.

These thought forms—and many others—stop the Universe from bringing the requests back. Not all the requests are fulfilled within a certain timeframe, and patience is lost. These thought forms are hidden deep in the 90 percent of the subconscious.

Electro-Magnetic Beings

People are electro-magnetic beings. Energy travels up and down the body through the nervous system, producing signals that magnetically send out and return thoughts, feelings, and emotions for life to be experienced. The energy centers work like doors that open and close for the energy to move in and out of.

Thoughts carry different frequencies, and based on the vibration of the thought, the energy centers will be opened or closed based on levels of acceptance and resistance in life. There are seven major energy centers in the body. Each center has a door that opens and closes, as well as a lock. This lock can be locked tight or unlocked. When the energy centers are closed and locked, the natural flowing energy is shut off from sending out the signals and stays in the individual energy field, creating discord. When these energy centers are open and unlocked, the energy is free-flowing to be expressed and received back in the best possible ways. The quality of these thoughts will determine the quality of the life experience from the energy that is sent.

Locking Doors

Negative or heavy thought forms keep the energy field around the body closed down and tight. When the energy field shrinks, feelings of depletion, drained, and exhaustion from stress sets in the body. These produce feelings such as anger, depression, and sadness. The energies of fear, doubt, and disbelief lock the energy doors. These three feelings keep the energy center locked tight and keep the heavy thought forms creating in the personal energy field. Over time, these energies will move into the body, causing ill health, dis-ease, and dis-function.

This is exactly what happened to me when I was working in the financial services industry. My energy centers were not being replenished with energy that was allowed to free flow through my body. The heavy thought forms that I was producing stagnated, and my digestion system was unable to digest food for several years. During this time with these heavy thought forms, I disconnected from my divine essence in the pursuit of money.

Being Graded

Karen had a job performance evaluation coming up. She knew her employer was going to review her performance, and the review would determine her raise. Consciously, Karen didn't realize that she started forming thoughts that were stopping the positive evaluation. She was an exceptional employee, but was worried.

Karen was unsure if she was performing up to her employer's standards and produced anxiety around being critiqued. Fear started to take over. Many of her thoughts included meeting expectations, meeting company goals, and feeling unlikable.

Karen recalled a previous time where she was so nervous in prior employment that when her performance evaluation was given, she learned that she didn't display the qualities that her employer desired in the job. Karen really hated the thought of being critiqued.

A Critical Mother

As it got closer to the review, Karen remembered her mother always being a critical person. Karen never felt like she could do anything right. She felt judged and unappreciated. When the performance review day arrived, Karen was so worried and full of fear that she was sick that day. As a result, she was released from her employment.

Triggers from Yesterday

Karen's past conditioning of life events created a scenario that she was familiar with through fear. Fear can be easily changed through a new mindset. Had Karen remembered that she was hired because the company believed that she was capable, confident, and had the abilities they were looking for, Karen would have received that raise.

There are two types of fear: instinctual fear and irrational fear. Instinctual fear is part of the genetic programming and survival mechanism designed to keep us safe and free from harm. Natural disasters, such as fires, earthquakes, or a hurricane will trigger instinctual fear to travel to safety. Other instinctual fears are when a robbery is taking place, shootings, or even coming across a bear while hiking.

What Karen experienced was an irrational fear. This type of fear is an absence of love and can be changed. The gift of irrational fear is designed to awaken to love, not live in absence of it. The subconscious mind will create programs to keep a feeling of safety, but the irrational fear is an illusion of feeling safe. With Karen's story, she wanted to feel safe from being criticized and how awful she felt growing up as a child, so the subconscious put in place the mechanism of fear to create the illusion of feeling safe. Karen closed the door to receiving the positive energy. Fears come in many forms, such as fear of rejection, fear of abandonment, or fear of being unlovable. These types of fears are all reprogrammable in the subconscious.

Questioning it All

Doubt is a feeling of uncertainty and indecision between belief and disbelief. Doubt is created when there is a belief that expectations outside of ourselves have to be met. These expectations are usually self-imposed limitations that are perceived from other people, which are not usually spoken out loud but felt. If the expectation is not expressed outwardly from the other person, then the expectations are only in our mind. It is through the attachment to the expectation that creates doubt allowing limiting thoughts.

Blake was looking for employment. He had been working as a banker and was passed over for a promotion. Blake was determined to move up the corporate ladder to the next tier. He applied for a job at a national banking firm and was preparing for the interview. He knew that he was the right fit for the job. He had the experience, the expertise, and clients who would follow him when he made the change. As the interview became closer, doubt came knocking on that door. Blake was passionate about his work and knew he had the experience, but started to wonder about the educational background that the national firm was requiring. The doubt allowed Blake to second guess his abilities. After all, his existing employer passed him over for a promotion that was long overdue. Some of his subconscious thoughts included, "Am I worthy of a higher paying career?" and "Maybe I don't have the education level required. Someone else with more education will receive the job."

STOP!

These doubt thoughts are creating an energy that will be brought into existence. Blake was setting himself up to not receive the new position because he created an energy of doubt. He doubted his education and wondered if it was "good enough" for the new company. Blake limited himself by shutting down the energy centers and locking his doors with doubt. Many times, we send out the energy signals to manifest and then, we allow doubt to lock the door and not allow the manifestation in.

When I was in financial services, I was responsible for hiring sales people to become securities licensed as financial advisors. Through the hiring process, the education level was considered, but experience always outweighed education. People with experience had a rich background of qualities that sometimes were not teachable because of their background. I considered people with education without experience, but that never was a deciding factor. Don't cancel the dreams and ideas with doubt because you second-guessed what an employer might be looking for. The good news is that when the doubt is transformed, the energy centers can unlock and freely open to allow the manifestations to come.

Unbelieving

Disbelief is the inability to accept truth and is usually used out of context. When these three words are spoken, *"I can't believe!"* and what is usually meant is "I believe!"

Julie had her house for sale for several months. She had received several offers, one being full price. Julie was super-excited about the full price offer and thought that family was perfect for the home she had lived in for so many years. Throughout the next several weeks, Julie exclaimed, "I can't believe that I got a full price offer!" The Universe is literal, and heard every word, especially the "I can't believe."

By using the phrase, "I can't believe", Julie created a pattern of disbelief. Slowly, the full price offer got reduced. What happened was Julie was exclaiming her joy by bringing in the subconscious energy of disbelief, and the manifestation that was asked for was cancelled. If Julie was able to express the joy without disbelief, such as "I am excited for my full price offer!", the end result would have manifested differently.

Changing the Locks

Fear, doubt, and disbelief work together. When one is present, the other two seem to follow. The good news is that we have the ability to change the locks by changing the energy behind the thought forms. When the locks are changed, a completely different outcome is created.

On a trip, I was crystal shopping in Mt. Shasta, and a friend asked if I had ever considered speaking on a cruise. The thought had never really been considered, but for a moment, I envisioned what it might look like speaking on a cruise. Two days after arriving home,

I received a phone call for a spiritual conference and wanted to know if I would come speak on their cruise.

I considered all the potential scenarios being on a large cruise ship, especially the weather out at sea. I worked through my fears, but I had one fear left when it was time to attend the cruise. My biggest fear was losing my cell phone in the middle of the Atlantic Ocean.

On a Cruise Ship

While on the cruise, mind thoughts such as "don't get too close to the railing taking pictures – if your phone falls in the water, the boat doesn't stop – you can't jump in after it – you are in the middle of the ocean." These thoughts continually played like a broken tape in my head, always there to remind me to be cautious with the phone.

Still, the vision of the cell phone falling into the ocean did not change. I did have a history of getting my phone wet and having it stop working. This was a new phone that I purchased to video record the presentation that I was giving on the cruise. My phone was also set up to conduct all the business I needed to do during this working vacation.

The day before my presentation – it happened! I was up on top of a submarine that was partially in the water taking pictures next to the railing, and my cell phone slid off the case and went into the ocean. My worst fear manifested into reality. I knew it was gone forever.

One of the guides on the submarine put on gear while the other one backed up the submarine to where the phone fell in. They assured me that this happens all the time, not to worry, and sometimes the phone was recovered. I was also informed that if the phone was recovered that it may not work again.

I panicked. I had fear. I doubted the recovery of my phone. New thoughts entered my mind about how to order a new phone when you didn't have a phone, alternatives for recording the presentations, and the thought of how would I communicate with anyone on the mainland.

In that moment, I made a decision that changed my reality instantly. I connected to my divine essence, chose to have faith that my phone would be recovered, releasing the doubt. A huge sense of peace came over me and the guide swam up with my phone. The phone had been in salt water for over seven minutes about 40 to 50 feet deep. I was in disbelief, but knew instantly that if I wanted the phone to work, I had to believe that it would.

Fresh water was poured all over the phone, and after it was dried off, my phone turned on and worked! The next day, the phone recorded the presentation. I learned valuable lessons that day. The first lesson was that nothing was ever truly lost from fear if you trusted the universal love force energy.

I also learned that trust, faith, and belief are powerful and would unlock those locks of fear, doubt, and disbelief.

CHAPTER 8

Thinking Sabotage

While fear, doubt, and disbelief lock the doors to your energy centers, there are several *after* thoughts that will close the doors to the energy centers as well. These are heavy thought forms that are hidden from our awareness called vices.

A vice is a negative thought form that is created to learn and grow from. If learning does not take place from the vice, they can become habits that self-sabotage the manifestations. These vices create the fuel for the self-sabotaging after thoughts to close the door and weaken the energy centers and stem from the fear, doubt, and disbelief.

A Type of Denial

Avoidance is keeping away, not doing something, or providing a temporary escape from someone or something. Procrastination leads to avoidance.

An example in money situations, avoidance happens when there is intention to delay paying bills. Holding onto money to the very last moment for a "just in case of emergency" scenario is a conditioned thought pattern. This can even be a habit when there is plenty of money for the expenses. If there is a limited amount of fixed income each month, this can be difficult to release the money to spend in the world.

Holding onto money and avoiding spending stops the flow of money and opportunities from returning to you. If the bill was already paid, a doorway opens, and the energy of money returns to you. This can show up as additional gifts, such as a friend buying you lunch or receiving a gift certificate to somewhere you enjoy. Sometimes, it is the very last dollar, but if that money is put out into circulation, then the opportunities for more to return will come back.

Finding Fault

Blaming is the next vice. Blaming is allowing another person to have power over us. There are decisions and choices that everyone makes in their day-to-day life, and blaming others gives the responsibility of that decision-making to someone else. When blaming happens, it is saying, "Here, take my power; I don't need it." An example of this is when a parent says to a child, "You make me so _____." In this scenario, the child was given the responsibility for how the parent chose to feel. The child received the blame, and this lowers their sense of worth in the moment. Often, advisors in the investment industry were blamed for clients' choices for mutual fund portfolio value when the fund didn't perform as expected. There were so many circumstances that affect a mutual fund value beyond the control of any advisor, such as fund selections and stock market trading. The advisor could only make a recommendation based on the goals of the client.

Blame is not always rational. When an individual choice is made, and it doesn't work out to the expectation, it is a natural tendency to cast blame. This is a hidden subconscious pattern. Once, I had a client contact me for some knee problems, blaming the celery juice they chose to drink.

A natural way to make decisions is through comparison, and judging is the vice. There are two types of judgment: observational and critical.

Observational judgment is neutral, meaning that identification can happen without feeling. There is not an emotional charge around the observation, and the process is used to make a decision. An example of an observational judgment is noticing that someone has on a green shirt. There is not an emotional charge, and the green shirt is used for identification purposes.

The second type of judgment that turns into a vice is critical judgment. This is where a personal opinion is expressed with the observation and becomes a negative emotional charge. The shirt might be green, but a disdain for neon lime green will be a critical judgment. This personal opinion may be different from another person.

Critical judgment will rob the happiness and joy inside.

Money Relativity

Judgments around money happen all the time. "How *much* does that cost? That is really expensive! That is a great bargain. Wow, that is cheap!" are some examples of money judgment. What is expensive for one person may not be expensive to another.

There are some independently wealthy people who think that a product $500 is a lot of money, while to someone else, that same product at $500 is a bargain. Judgment has nothing to do with financial success, but with everything on the viewpoint of money. In the financial world, judgment is also a double-edged sword. Not only is it used to determine the difference between right and wrong (judges do this for a profession), money judgments can be placed against people and property, such as liens.

That's a Strong Word

The opposition of love is hate, a very strong vice. This is a strong, passionate dislike directed at certain groups, individuals, or situations. When hate is expressed outwardly, there needs to be realization that the hate was inside, waiting to be expressed outside. This energy surfaces when a person does not feel appreciated or they feel unheard. If the feeling of non-appreciation is true, then money will not appreciate. Remember, what is on the inside will reflect back on the outside. What happens with the energy of hate is that the emotional needs are not being met, triggering the emotional feelings of deep anger and resentment.

The energy of hate will stop the flow of all the good to be received rather quickly. If hate is the energy being sent out, the energy field around the body constricts, and the people around you can feel that. As a result, they may come into your business and purchase, and they definitely won't refer new people to you. Just the mere thought, *I hate paying my bills*, will stop the energy flow and start creating chaos in your life.

All About You

Egotism is another vice that you need to be aware of. There is a difference between ego and egotism. Ego is an identity that gives a description of who you are, such as your name. Egotism is a little different. This is where people only consider themselves, wanting to elevate to feel better.

This kind of pride is taking the fame and fortune at the expense of someone else. We could see egotism in the workforce when a manager, supervisor, or team lead takes all the credit for a project when the team worked on it together and credit was not passed down.

The sharing of the recognition and appreciation of a job well done didn't happen. This is an energetic boastful taking energy to feel more powerful, valued, or elevated, keeping others underneath, creating arrogance.

Disapproval based on a perceived fault or mistake is criticism. Criticism, including constructive criticism, looks outwardly to others for approval, validation, and advice, but when met with a contradiction, it forms a vice. The other person serves as a filter to give feedback.

Sophisticated Put Downs

Criticism is designed to assist in changing behavior, making things better and stronger. There are hidden patterns with criticism. Personal opinion on how much money someone is perceived to have, or too little, is a criticism. There is often an association with money and the spiritual work someone may or may not have done.

The viewpoint of people having riches without "having done" their spiritual work, is a criticism. "I don't understand how this person can have all this money – they haven't done their spiritual inner work!" was what a client said to me once. This is based on a perception through a filter when the truth is, there is not an understanding on what happened for that person to acquire money.

Criticism is a way to attempt to avoid lack-generated feelings inside of the essence. Every time a criticism of another person is engaged in, the Universe not knowing the intent behind the energy vibration signal sent out, criticism returns back and keeps it in the energy field.

Defensiveness becomes the fuel and starts breaking down the energy field, leaving a feeling of depletion inside. Since money and the energy field are both forms of energy, when one area is affected, the other area follows. Staying in criticism will close the energy door and block all the abundance that is meant for you.

Envy

Jealousy is an enormous block to receiving abundance. Showing envy of another person regarding their material items, achievements, or advantages will keep a state of lack energy inside. Jealousy is a wanting of what others have, creating a neediness inside. This takes the energy of another to try and fill up the void inside, rather than going to the source energy to receive is.

Greed is the opposite of jealousy. Greed is keeping and hoarding, preventing others from having it. Both of these are vices that are equally damaging from two different points of view. People become jealous and greedy with others through the want of materialism, money, personal looks, or spiritual gifts. The result is that the energy flow stops. Jealousy and greed create a poor self-image, feelings of intimidation by others, and competition occurs. These two vices, when accepted, offer feelings of internal insecurity, and money is sought after for external security. A subconscious pattern begins. Insecurity will feed the fear, feelings of inadequacy and anger can surface and then a downhill spiral begins. Remember that phrase, green with envy?

Lost in the Past

The last vice is regret. "I wish I coulda, woulda, shoulda." Regret is holding accountable the *past* action with future information that was not available at the time when the decision was made. Regret breeds buyers' remorse when the best possible decision was made with the information and knowledge at the time the decision was made.

If the decision was made several weeks later, the decision-making process may have had a different outcome. This does not mean that waiting is needed to make a decision, but only to recognize that when decisions are made, the best decision was made at that time it was made.

Regret happens more than realized. When those words of, "I wish I coulda, woulda, shoulda" are thought or spoken, this is the beginning of regret. Buyer's remorse happens more frequently with large purchases, such as purchasing a new car. The current car is worn out, hardly runs, you are always repairing it, and winter is on the way. The decision is made, and a new car is in order.

The budget is figured out for how much to pay for the new car, how much can be afforded for the car payment, and the new car is purchased. Then, the next week, your furnace breaks, and the money saved already went towards a new car. The hidden energy of regret enters and, "I wish I coulda, woulda, shoulda" made that decision differently.

This is 20/20

A part of the energy field just got stuck in the past of the decision that was made, while being in the present moment, while creating the future. However, fully moving into the future moment is impossible, since a part of the energy field is stuck with regret. Holding on to regret is a way for the subconscious to attempt to keep us safe from repeating future mistakes. After all, hindsight is 20/20.

Just like driving a car, looking forward is the goal of driving safely into the future. Glancing backward may keep awareness, but releasing the regret will allow for safe forward movement of life experiences. Unlimited abundance has a greater capacity to manifest when the full essence of being-ness is available.

CHAPTER 9

The Monkey Man

Perched on the shoulders sits *the Monkey Man*, whose job is to hold every possible burden. These burdens are heavy energy thought forms such as avoidance, hate, egotism, and jealousy. The more that is held onto, the less prosperity flows into life.

The Monkey Man added secret locks of fear, doubt, and disbelief to ensure that his job stays intact. Without these burdens, the Monkey Man is without employment. Every burden steals a portion of internal happiness and joy. The body begins to crumble under the added weight carrying all of the heavy-feeling forms.

Paying the Price

The Monkey Man also expects payment for the services that are performed. Acceptable forms of payment include our health and well-being, reducing our financial resources for health providers from the effects of the added stress. Other forms of payment include personal relationships dissolving and holding on to regret and jealousy.

The Monkey Man will even squander away the savings that were built up, blaming others for the choices that were made while criticizing and judging.

It is time to release the Monkey Man from the job of holding onto every heavy thought form. As each of the Monkey Man's vices relinquish, the physical body becomes lighter, and piece by piece, the internal state of happiness and joy returns. As the additional weight is removed, health returns, and prosperity and love come rushing into the life experience. All areas of life start to become magnified. Soon, the Monkey Man has disappeared and vanished, by releasing the self-sabotaging *after*-thoughts.

Mind Whispering

Releasing the Monkey Man involves the process of mind whispering. The process starts with a door lock. The next step is to identify the vice and how the vice feels inside. The last step is to identify the light feeling that would rather be experienced. This process is similar to when you compared the lower feelings with direct the desired higher feelings you did earlier with the direct experience with money, except that you are adding the door lock and vice that keeps the energy centers blocked from receiving abundance.

Application

You should look at some of your Monkey Man burdens that are being held. This can be something directly experienced or an experience someone projected that was accepted.

The door locks are fear, doubt, and disbelief. Vices are: avoidance, blame, judgment, hate, criticism, egotism, jealousy or greed, or regret.

When you read these words, say them out loud one by one, and see what kind of emotional triggers appear. You can see what personal experiences are attached to each of these words.

Now, look at these connecting experiences again from the higher feeling perspective. Can you do that? I actually have a whole interactive program and workbook to assist with this. Go to *www. dawnacampbell.com/financially-fit*.

Repeat the exercise for every door lock and vice. This will start the process of releasing the self-sabotaging *after* thoughts to become Financially Fit.

3 Keys to Increasing Prosperity

Where the focus is creates experiences in life. Staying focused on the vices of the self-sabotaging *after* thoughts, the manifestations are canceled, because the wrong type of fuel was used. The good news is every lock has a key. Imagine the front door of a house with a lock on it. In order to go inside, a key is needed to unlock the door.

The energy center works the same way. In order for the manifestation energy to enter, the proper key must be used to unlock the energy center. Having an unlocked energy center will get the energy flowing again. The keys that are needed to unlock the doors of fear, doubt, and disbelief are faith, trust, and belief.

Faith

Faith unlocks the door of doubt. Faith allows the unseen energy that is sent out to the Universe be made seen and manifest into existence. Unseen energy that leaves the body is the formless energy field, or divine essence. Love is the divine essence that Albert Einstein called the Universal Energy of Love. This energy is measurable in every cell of the body and is called Adenosine Triphosphate, or ATP. This is where the currency of life resides. ATP is a high-energy molecule whose job is to store and supply the cells with needed energy from the food and nutrients that are consumed. The divine essence also needs food to feed the soul or spirit energetically, and the food is faith.

Faith is also a financial term that is used by many. "In good faith" is one of them. Deposits of money are recorded, in good faith, when there is an intention to make a large purchase, such as a house using an escrow account. Faith allows the expression of truth to be released from the energy field to come into form. In good faith uses money as one way to express this truth.

Trust

Trust is an allowing of what is asked for to come into the reality of the experience that was asked for. Trust is the key that unlocks fear. Love is the divine essence, which is why it is called the Universal Force of Love, and fear is not a part of that equation. To dissolve the fear, trust is needed.

Trusting that the manifestation requests are heard and that the Universe will bring the very things that are asked for. This happens when a complete alignment takes place with the divine essence. To be trustworthy is to be someone who can be trusted.

Financial terms also include the word "trust". When property is given to another person, they become a trustee. They are entrusted with the material items or financial accounts. A trust is also a legal document where the trustee manages the property. The trustee is the person who distributes the property according to the instructions in the trust.

Some trusts are generational and ongoing from family to family and take the place of a will, which hands over the property to the surviving family members, charities, or other organizations. Money is even printed with the words "In God we Trust."

Belief

Beliefs empower to create and move forward with life. What is believed is the truth about ourself and leaves the energy field to create the outside world. Beliefs are convictions of truth that are felt as a divine essence of your being. What the personal beliefs are on the inside is also how we interact with money. Every person's belief is an expression of individual truth and gives focused direction in choices of creating. There is not a right or wrong in which beliefs to believe in, only an experience that is created where a gift can be discovered.

Belief is the key that unlocks disbelief. The emotional charge gives the belief of the fuel to allow the existence. There are many beliefs about money that are given throughout history and religion that is deeply encoded in the subconscious.

Money beliefs can either be positive or negative in nature. Positive money beliefs will allow money to come into existence and multiply. Positive money beliefs include, "I am worthy of money", "money effortlessly comes into existence for me", and "I am prosperous in every business transaction."

Negative beliefs about money gives the belief fuel also, but prevents money from coming into existence. Some examples are "I never have enough money," "money is the root of all evil," or "money doesn't grow on trees."

The Right Combination

These three keys work together like a combination that opens a safe. The right numbers are needed, in the right sequence, or the lock stays locked. Here, faith, trust, and belief are interconnected and can be used in any combination. When there is faith, you believe that there is a foundational truth inherent to the divine essence.

When there is trust and faith through what is believed will be experienced. When there is belief, a conviction of truth, trust and faith are automatic, and the proper energy fuel is applied for manifesting. These three keys—trust, faith, and belief—will unlock the doors to the energy centers and create what is believed in.

How does this combination work together? Yes, all three are needed to have the right combination, otherwise the manifestation will not come into existence. This combination is needed to have the formless energy create the form.

My Teenager's Phone

My daughter, Jessica, who was about 15 at the time, had a cell phone. As she was using the phone, it fell in a cup of lemonade and stopped working. As a teenager, her entire life had been cut off. After a few days of complete sadness, she was determined to have her cell phone work again. Jessica had faith; she believed that it would turn on and trusted that it would be true. When she applied the combination, the phone turned on and worked.

Jessica had never been so excited, and many days' worth of friends' messages started appearing. On the first phone call, she went to exclaim her excitement and said the canceling words "I can't believe", and the Universe heard, and cancelled the working phone immediately.

A person doesn't need to have the same set of beliefs as another person to have the desired outcome as long as faith and trust are present. A friend of mine believed so strongly that if they ordered their steak medium in a restaurant, that it was always cooked to perfection to the desired outcome of medium rare.

The thought process behind this was that chefs were trained to undercook the meat, because if it was overcooked, nothing could be done about it, except cook a new steak.

This belief enforced the faith and trust in the belief that they had. I had never considered this perspective before. I believe that if you order a steak medium rare, the chef would cook it accordingly. Which person was right in the belief? Both. It is due to the combination of faith and trust with the belief that allows the manifestation to return.

CHAPTER 10

Prosperity Doors

Once the keys are used to unlock the energy center, the doors need to be opened to allow the energy to flow through. Where vices closed the doors, virtues open the doors. Virtues are moral positive characteristics that are principles to live by.

These qualities create positive feelings that enhance the thought forms to attract the good things life has to offer. The good things include: wealth, abundance, and prosperity in all areas of life that also affect health and relationships. When virtues are in alignment with thoughts and feelings, all things become possible, and instant thought form creation happens.

Expectations and Energy Fields

When the doors are open, the electrical energy flows outwardly, creating a vibrational alignment magnetically attracting back the requests that were sent out. When these thought energy patterns are enhanced with positive feelings, the energy field expands, allowing more to be received. This is how the universal law of attraction is used by the virtues.

Calm is a Superpower

The first virtue is peace, a keeping of a strong, calm, and tranquil inner self when faced with obstacles to overcome. Peace is a freedom from disturbance and absent of conflict. Benefits include stress reduction and discord in life. Peace opens the energy door to allow prosperity for creation. Energy flowing in includes: money, financial stability, abundance, and wealth, which are all forms of creation energy. Having a "piece of the pie" is a way to have a share in profits of business.

Between Worlds

Balance is having the ability of being content and is the center point between the material world and the spiritual world. The scales are equal or proper distribution of weight, allowing the material success to come into existence through spiritual success.

When the thoughts, feelings, and emotions are in a balanced state, a state of steadiness and security in the financial world with money is the result. If an area is not in balance, instability can easily happen. Flamingos balance gracefully and beautifully on one leg. Be like a flamingo.

Balance also allows the creativity and passion to flow through the door, increasing prosperity. Balance is a way to monetize the creations that are brought into existence, and don't forget to balance the bank account or check your balance sheets.

This Brings Good Fortune

The feeling of experiencing great pleasure is joy opens this energy center up with the happiness that can be expressed out to the world. The energy of joy brings good fortune and the prospects of possessing the material things that are desired. This includes all abundance, successful undertakings, and profitable joint ventures.

Joy is the fuel that is needed to feed the energy body to allow proper nourishment for the physical body. Receiving money allows a feeling of joy to enter our energy field. Just watch a child when they receive their first dollar, an allowance for completing extra jobs or chores. The expression can be priceless, and a sense of worth increases. This is what compensation for service rendered is designed to do: allow for the energy of joy.

This Holds it All Together

The nest virtue is a state of being, that divine essence that is the universal force called love. This is the essence that connects the mind, body, and soul together like glue. Love is a formless energy, and yet, forms all things. The energy of love is an incredible tender, soft, and nurturing energy. If you look at dollar bills, they are printed with "for legal tender of all debts, public and private".

Love is the legal tender spiritually for all debts. The perfect love frequency can be measured at 528 hertz. This is the miracle frequency that repairs all DNA and is the healing. When a state of pure love is invoked at this frequency, the bliss of instant creation can exist. Love is the pathway to find meaning in life and opens the door for all things to being possible.

Being Thankful

The feeling and verbally communicating appreciation for people, circumstances, and material possessions is the energy of gratitude. As gratitude increases, so does appreciation. One of the main words used to describe how money grows and increases is by appreciation.

The first step is to really grow the inner appreciation of the divine essence through the virtue of gratitude. The energy then flows out of us, into the energy field, and magnifies the outside world, which in return appreciates in volume and value. Gratitude allows the present moment to be cherished and the feeling of being abundant. When gratitude is expressed, the fullness of the experience can be expressed. One way in the money world that gratitude is expressed is when exceptional service is received, a money gratuity is often given.

Spiritual Alignment

Harmony aligns the mind, body, and soul in a certain vibrational frequency that harmonizes. Think about a finely tuned instrument playing a beautiful melody. When the incorrect note is played, you can hear it. The note is disharmonious to the rest of the music. Each of the organs inside the body produces a sound that is in harmony to each other and with the divine essence.

When disharmony is in the body, discomfort, pain, depression, and anxiety can develop inside through the stress function. Keeping in tune with the body, alleviating the stress, keeps a strong body and energy field producing harmony. Keeping in harmony will bring in financial harmony and freedom.

More than Pretty

Beauty is a combination of qualities that gives intense pleasure and deep satisfaction for the mind. Divine blessings are the result. Beauty is the reminder of the nature of existence and the origin of divine essence. When this remembering takes place, new energy doors open, and infinite creations can be experienced. Beauty can be synonymous with consciousness and the more that is perceived, the more that is projected.

Beauty is in the eye of the beholder. How money is seen and viewed will bring in the feeling patterns of either the intense pleasure or despair for the satisfaction of the mind.

Be a Truth Seeker

Truth is the last virtue. Truth aligns the inner feelings and thoughts with the outward actions, living life in the most authentic way. Truth allows sincerity in action. When living in truth, the direct experience of the feelings validates the existence by how it returns to you.

When the truth is lived in accordance with the divine essence, your direct thought experience will instantly create. With money, how to think and feel about you on the inside will be how the money resonates with you on the outside. Every person's truth is different. Here are some examples with money:

- A person who is kind will be kind with their money.
- A person who is a gambler will gamble their money.
- A person who is stressed will have stress with their money.
- A person who is mindful will be mindful about their money.

Application

In the previous exercise, you uncovered the vice that was experienced and the feeling behind it to transform to a higher feeling that was desired based on what was missing or needed in the event that was recorded in the subconscious.

Look to see what corresponding virtues you might be discovering from your experience.

Looking at the list of virtues, close your eyes and really feel the virtue with the higher feelings and go deeper. When sitting within the energy of the virtue and the higher feeling, experience the bliss of the divine essence inside. This helps bring to the previous event the new balance inside to create from a higher perspective.

Pivot and Shift

This strategy was taught to me from the Medicine Woman. She taught me that if you are in a room and there are energies that you don't like, meaning people have a negative attitude, you can physically move, changing the energy of the room.

On a physical level, you only have to change your position, stand up and get a glass of water, or maybe even leave the room. Every movement that is used will energetically change the physical energy of the room. This can be applied to the emotional level as well.

Here is how it works. Review the first events you can recall about money taught to you growing up. Then, I want you to rewrite the event from the higher perspective of the positive feeling and virtue of the experience that you wrote down above. This is called a pivot and shift, recording the feeling energy that was the fuel to a different fuel.

The events of the experience do not change, but you are pivoting and shifting the experience you had before "unsticking yourself" by the new perspective. When the higher feeling comes in, there is a new hormone balance that happens inside the body that reprograms the energy field, the cellular memory, and sends out a different vibrational frequency to the world.

CHAPTER 11

Opening and Closing Doors

The energy centers are called Chakras, a Sanskrit word for wheel or disk. A Chakra is a spinning wheel of light that moves the energy from inside through the physical body, into the energy field. This energy is the divine essence and is composed of the conscious and subconscious thoughts.

This energy produced both a frequency and vibration of thoughts, feelings, and emotions to create a life experience. There are seven major chakras that send out the encoded energy of information about the essence of who and what we are. Each chakra spins a different frequency producing a sound, light, and color for an energetic reading of the information that is sent out.

Swinging Doors

The Chakra works like a door. When the experience is a negative thought or feeling, the door shuts and the energy field around the body shrinks. When the experience is positive, the door opens and the energy field expands. A normal range for the energy field is 3 -6 feet around the outside of the body.

The first 3 chakras relate to the physical & material world. These 3 chakras keep us grounded while creating physical form in the material world. The top 3 chakras connect energy to the spiritual world. This is the formless energy that is used to bring into existence the form of manifesting. The center chakra is the heart, the bridge that is the energy essence we all must pass through to bring the ideas of creation into form.

The **Root Chakra** is the bottom energy center. This chakra is the foundation, the beliefs that were experienced growing up, the tribal beliefs, and social conditioning. This chakra is at the base of the spine, where we sit at the base of the spine, and where the abundance starts to flow in. Avoidance closes this abundance door while peace opens it.

The second energy center is called the **Sacral Chakra** and is located behind the belly button. This chakra center is the relationship to everything on the outside including relationships with other people, money, sex, home, or business, the seat of creation. Creation is on many levels but is the form that is experienced on the material plane. The block that stops this door from being open is blame, while balance is opening the door.

The **Solar Plexus**, sun center, is the power center. This chakra is about personal power, empowerment, and the relationship to your inner strength on the inside. The Solar Plexus is located where the stomach is and takes in food internally to give the body the nutritional fuel needed to create with. Judgment keeps this door shut while joy allows the door to open.

The **Heart Chakra** is our bridge between the physical and spiritual world. The heart is the intersecting node of these two worlds. This bridge is what must be crossed to bring the ideas and inspiration into action and form physically. The heart chakra is the love center that resonates to a frequency of 528 hertz. This is the energy that repairs the DNA and is a miracle tone for healing. This is the energy that Albert Einstein called the Universal Force of Love. The essence came from this energy and will return to this energy one day. While on the physical plane, this frequency is accessible and is the signal that can be sent out to attract the manifestations. Hate keeps this center locked up tight while love expands the energy keeping the door wide open.

How we express ourselves comes through the **Throat Chakra**. This gives the ability to speak verbally creating the thoughts expressed out loud. This verbal expression allows the creation to be transformed into existence. When criticism and egotism are expressed, this door stays shut and the energy can't flow back. To open this center, expression of gratitude and harmony will bring appreciation and abundance.

The **Third-Eye Chakra** allows the dream and vision to be seen and dreamed of before the creations come into form. Visualizing, this center gives the gift of spiritual sight to see with clarity and to assist moving into the future with goals and dreams. This center is located at the pineal gland, near the center of the brain, often represented as an "eye" between the two eyebrows. Jealousy and greed keeps the sight clouded and closed. To have this door open, seeing everything through the eyes of beauty is acknowledged. Here, we have the capacity to see divinity.

The last chakra is the **Crown Chakra**. This is where thought creation happens and gives a sense of knowing. This center is located at the top of the head, the crown. When the crown is accessed, we have the ability to access all of what we are. When the crown chakra is accessed through meditation, a theta brain wave is produced and if deep enough, the thought can detach and has the freedom to move through the universe faster than the speed of light, and return instant thought creation However, regret keeps the door shut and stuck in the past, while living in truth keeps the door open. The truth shall set you free is all about taking action in accordance with the divine self.

The Locks and Keys

The door can be locked when it is shut. The door locks are Fear, Doubt, and Disbelief. If the door needs to be unlocked, the keys to opening those doors are Faith, Trust and Belief.

Lock	Key
Fear	Trust
Doubt	Faith
Disbelief	Belief

Staying in the energy of faith, trust, and belief and virtuous feelings, unlimited creations happen and all things become possible. Each one of these locks intersects the chakras, as well as the keys. When all of the doors are open, and the energy is freely moving up and down, the overall pattern that is formed is a figure 8 patterns that resembles a DNA strand.

In numerology, 8 is the sign of abundance and infinity. DNA is the divine blueprint. The divine essence is encoded with this frequency of abundance and prosperity through the DNA, the blueprint for life. The only requirement to have accessing this divine right to abundance is to stay in virtue while standing firm with the 3 keys, Faith, Trust, and Belief, and this is how we stay Financially Fit.

Beautiful Heart Energy

One of the purposes on the material plane that I believe in is the ability to create a beautiful heart. Here is a meditation that I wrote to assist in releasing the blocked energy that shuts the energy doors while bringing in the three keys to increasing your prosperity and virtues to keep the door open.

Creating a Beautiful Heart Meditation

I recognize that I am a vibrational energy field and that everywhere I am, I infuse love. Any vibrational frequency that is not of the highest vibrations that enters my energy field, I am impervious to, and I release it to the light to transform back to the Universal Love Force Energy to me.

I release and relinquish fear, unworthiness, guilt, victimhood, being taken advantage of, and avoidance. I restore peace, calmness, and stillness in myself, and send the energy of peace and serenity everywhere I am. I have the ability to stand in peace. (Root Chakra)

I release and relinquish blame, judgment, criticism, gossip, scarcity, and physical and emotional pain. I restore the connection to my creativity and expression of new ideas of ideas, creating a new energy flow through balanced masculine and feminine energies, with life being plentiful. I have the ability to create balance. (Sacral Chakra)

I release and relinquish doubt, disbelief, uncertainty, chaos, separation, isolation, feeling alienated, feeling alone, being manipulated, and feeling rejected. I restore my happiness, joy, personal empowerment, my ability to generate action through the universal love force energy with courage, bravery, honor, respect, and dignity. I have the ability to be the joy. (Solar Plexus Chakra)

I release and relinquish hate, war, poverty, loneliness, betrayal, dislike, revenge, and holding grudges. I restore love, compassion, forgiveness, hope, strength of health, the healing miracle frequency of 528 hertz, and to know that love, the healing power is the divine healing of the Universal Love Force Energy that we call Creator. With every breath that I breathe, I have the ability to feel the love. (Heart Chakra)

I release and relinquish stress, worry, egotism, panic, sickness, illness, disease, negative karma, and radiation. I restore gratitude, my needs being met, allowing the harmony of life to flow in increasing our positive vibrational communication of integrity and honesty. I am always connected to the Universal Love Force Energy field. I have the ability to speak with gratitude and hear harmony. (Throat Chakra)

I release and relinquish illusion, dishonesty, jealousy, greed, and heavy thought forms, such as anger, frustration, and rage. I restore my inner vision of divine living, beauty, increased intuition, nurturing oneness with all of life, all of creation and clarity. I have the ability to see the beauty of life. (Third Eye Chakra)

I release and relinquish abandonment, regret, and resistance. I restore truth, knowledge, wisdom, purity, and to know that my body and the earth that I live on is a healing temple through faith, trust, and belief. I have the ability to live in truth. (Crown Chakra)

My Personal Mantra

When I was going through the downturn of my health, my relationship ending, and financial devastation, I was using various forms of meditation. While in meditation, I was given a personal mantra that I repeat often, especially when times feel overwhelming. This mantra always brings me a sense of well-being and an internal knowing that everything is okay. I share this with you.

> Trust, and you will see.
> Believe, and you will know.
> Have faith, all is well.
> Follow your heart and
> spirit will lead you.

CHAPTER 12

Money & Sex

There is an old debated question of which came first, the chicken or the egg? The question is the same, money or sex? When the energy centers open and aligned, both *money and sex* flow effortlessly. How you interact with every relationship outside you is how all of your creations interact with other people.

Creating happens a number of different ways; through sex, money, people, environments, and places. To fully understand the complete dynamics of the relationship between money and sex, it is important to understand how the first two energy centers—the root and sacral—interact with money and sex.

Root Chakra, Money, and Sex

The root chakra gives us information and structure about our tribe that we belong to. This is the family that we are born into and raised. This energy center is the strength of survival instinct and the family needs. Social conditioning and community beliefs about housing, clothing, food, and shelter are also dominant in this energy center. Without this energy center, the physical world would not come into existence.

Throughout history, the previous generations before had sex for procreation and to carry out a family legacy. Sex was a duty and an obligation from a root chakra point of view. Much of this viewpoint was handed down through the philosophy of the churches and various religions. Reproduction was considered the only acceptable form of having intercourse.

Most everyone lived in survival mode, allowing for only the physical needs to be met. These experiences and beliefs are passed down through the generations to have all the survival needs met first. They farmed the land, needed help, so they had sex to procreate, and children were the result. Farming the land turned into money creation if the crops or animals were sold or bartered for their needs. What wasn't sold, was kept to provide for the needs of the family to survive on.

Once the physical and material needs are met, the sacral chakra energy can open up. This transition from the root chakra focus to the sacral chakra changes the perspective from "me" to "us". This is the shift from being an individual to a relationship. Coming out of survival mode, the emotional needs can start being met.

The Seat of Creation

The sacral chakra energy center is considered the Seat of Creation. This center opens up the emotional component that is needed to create. We have several choices in how to create when this energy is alive and moving through us. Creation can happen through sex by having children, or by money by creating businesses.

The seat of creation is creating a relationship with ourselves, a relationship with others, relationship with money, home, businesses, lovers, social life, community, including the creation of new life. The main two ways we create from this center is through money or sex, sometimes both.

Since the seat of creation opens up an emotional component to create from, this is where things can be confused between our essence and money because of the amount of emotion that is applied. Money and sex creates a strong energy bond to emotion and creation.

To have the ability to attract the abundance and prosperity that is desired, this energy center needs to be in balance and alignment. Realizing the strengths and weaknesses as it relates to creating is helpful. When the energy center door is opened and aligned, the energy center door is opened and can move freely in and out. When the door is shut, the energy doesn't move through, and weaknesses show up.

The strengths that come to and open the door to the seat of creation include financial stability, the ability to take risks—including financial risks, opportunities, and having the ability to recover from a loss. Decision-making abilities are also a strength to the balanced energy center, which create having choices in life both personally and professionally.

When the seat of creation is unbalanced, the weaknesses show up. Feeling a loss of control, being controlled by another person, or realizing a financial loss has a large impact. Feeling dominated over by another person can also close the door down to the energy center. Addictions, betrayal, and abandonment can trigger an imbalance as well.

Abuse is anything that diminishes a person's sense of worth and includes physical, emotional, sexual, or financial will also weaken this energy center.

Money Manipulation

Money, power, and sex all lead to a form of control. Having money can be used just as easily to control another as a lack of money. In relationships, often the person who has the money controls the relationship, including the sexual nature of the relationship. Money has such an emotional power that feeling or being controlled is accepted.

There is an interesting dynamic with partnerships and control. The control is a fight for dominance when a person feels threatened. A martial pattern that occurs with clients is that whomever controls the money flow also controls the sex. The spouse then used judgment and criticism as vices to fight to gain back their sense of control.

The other way this surfaces is when one partner is the main wage earner or receives an inheritance, the other partner feels an inadequacy. By pointing out the flaws and judging them in another is a way to gain a sense of control and importance. This dynamic is also the same for business partnerships and joint ventures where an inequality is felt.

A healthy functioning exchange process is a service paid for, so giving of resources is required, in exchange for the services being provided. This changes to a form of control when giving is only to get back. Money is being used to manipulate the other person to receive back what they want. In this sense, money is being used to buy a favor. This imbalance occurs when the exchange is not perceived as equitable on both sides. Manipulation also occurs when others want to be around only because the bill is paid when they are with you.

Controlling Money Thoughts

With couples, the need to feel loved and nurtured with the partner is so strong that there is an attempt to control to get back those needs. This happens when money is used to feel loved and nurtured. These thoughts create unhappiness out of a need to control. Here are some client scenarios that came from hidden controlling thought forms.

The miserable job is the only way to make money, and the spouse agrees.

Yes, everyone has a need for money, but agreeing that this is the only job to have for money bringing misery is where the control comes in. There are many jobs out there that can provide happiness. The agreeing spouse is keeping an energetic control over the partner to feel a certain way, so they feel better about themself. This form of control is a type of egotism.

The divorce is 100 percent the spouse's fault, therefore there is not equal division of assets.

This does happen more often than realized. The assets are divided based on percentage of fault, and are used to control the other party to obtain money. This form of control brings up the vice of blaming. All of the responsibility for the breakup is on the other person. Relationships take two people, otherwise, it would not be a relationship.

The partner tries to help the spouse earn more money.

Whether or not there is a need for additional income, the partner views that the spouse is inadequate in earning additional income. They want to help, but it results in controlling behavior. This is the vice of criticism coming out. When overly criticized for not earning income, even if they help, only leaves the partner with resentment when it doesn't happen.

Giving the spouse a "to-do" list for a job search.

This creates a lack of trust for the spouse to do it themselves. Trust is a door lock that keeps the money energy center locked down tight. There is a fine line between encouraging and wanting to do it for them. Each person is responsible to take action to create. The spouse may have a different process in finding a job than the partner. By giving them a to-do is saying "let me do it for you, because you are incapable," and lack of trust is the result.

CHAPTER 13

Gender Views

Men and women view money and sex differently. Some of these views are from the culture that we live in, the genetics we are born with, and social conditioning. Hormonal balances based on the amount of testosterone and estrogen that is being produced in the body is also a factor.

Depending if the left side or the right side of the brain is more dominant, this will demonstrate how money is used to create. Here, the terms man and woman are being used only to make a distinction based on brain dominance.

Generally speaking, men tend to view money as a means for freedom and power. They compete with and for money. The social currency for a man is professional and financial success. Men will also trade money for sex, regardless of the context of the relationship.

In a marriage, the man will provide money, security, and protection for emotional support and a place to come home to. Money in the male brain represents autonomy and freedom, an individual perspective. This also alludes to power and control, which can result in hoarding or saving.

Women, on the other hand, view money as safety and security. The social currency of a woman is youth, beauty, charm, and sexuality.

Woman will naturally trade sex for security. In a marriage, the woman will provide babies, a warm and nurturing place, and sex to feel security and protected through the man providing and working. The feminine brain with money is emotional, tending to shop and spend. Generosity is considered a form of love.

Most of the Time Truths

Regardless of gender, both are looking for love. The "I love you" for him is wanting good sex, and for her, the "I love you" is financial security. The basic need of love drives an instinctual behavior to bond together, even if the motivations are different.

Genetically, men are the hunters to bring home the food, and women are the gatherers who prepare it. When it comes to relationships, there has been a growing trend for women to take over and hunt for the man who will bring home the bacon. If you find yourself in this role, you will always be hunting, even after you capture the man wondering where the bacon is. Through social conditioning, many of the traditional roles have been mixed up like this. Women can be wage earners while the man stays home taking care of the family. Using both sides of the brain are equally important when it comes to money viewpoints.

Money and Sexual Intimacy

Money has the power to replace sexual intimacy, since both are vulnerable topics. There is such an emotional charge for people around money that feelings of inadequacy, obsessions with accumulation, and disgust with materialism can result. All of this affects the health of sexual intimacy. People want to feel an emotional closeness with another person. Money and sex provides this connectedness. Sex is usually the intimacy that is sought, however, the person who controls the money controls the sex.

Intimacy is deeper than the act of sex or creating money. "Into me see" is another way to look at forming a deep bond and interconnectedness with your partner. Forgiveness is a deep, intimate act, "for-giving" yourself and others releases the emotional baggage that was being held onto though those vices.

In a true intimate relationship, there is an enjoyment of sharing time together, and happiness comes first. Being honest and open about meeting needs brings a good foundation of communication to the relationship. There is a give-give in the relationship, allowing both to receive. With intimacy, trust is developed in making the right choices and detaching from the outcome.

Money can facilitate avoidance for true emotional sexual intimacy. People avoid relationships, believing that a certain level of money has to be achieved first. Money is being substituted for emotional intimacy through the avoidance of relationships.

Money and Sexual Energy

There is a correlation between sexual flow and financial flow. Basically, more sex equals more abundance. Sexual energy is experiencing pleasure with life and feeling good. When we feel good, we attract goodness. This energy will build up inside and keep building until it is released. If the sexual energy is not used to create babies, it does need to be channeled somewhere.

The inner sexual energy is such a strong force of creation that it does influence the rest of the human energies. Prosperity is one of those energies that comes from within and can be greatly influenced by how sexual energy is handled. How the creative force of sexual energy is channeled through the body will determine the level of magnetism that is developed in the energy body.

Attraction Power

Charisma is the magnetic personal quality and is a powerful attraction when the sexual energy is balanced. Increases in confidence, optimism, enthusiasm, and communication—both verbal and nonverbal—are all a part of charisma. This attractor can lead to business opportunities and activities that are bound to appear. When the sexual energy is channeled through as a force of creation, the personal attractiveness increases, and returns the abundance.

When the sexual energy is blocked and no longer flowing, the abundance and prosperity in life also stops flowing. Ancient cultures knew about the powerful creative force that is inside, and when a woman's partner crossed over, another stepped in to take the role, so the creative force wouldn't die.

Having sex just to have sex doesn't work either, or at least it's rarely sustainable over long periods of time. This depletes the creative energy, rather than amplifies it. There is a delicate balance.

Aligning with the Seat of Creation, releasing the blocked energy to enhance your prosperity is the next principle to becoming financially fit.

Releasing Blocked Sexual Energy

Trauma and abuse that has been experienced in life will block the flow of sexual energy. How you feel about sex, what your parents and educators taught you about sex, and your experiences with sex will also determine how the creative force is within in.

These feelings can be released and reprogrammed using the process and can open the energy center to receive.

HERE IS A SAMPLE FROM MY WORKBOOK AND PRIVATE COACHING PROGRAM…

My parents, grandparents, siblings, and teachers taught me:

_____

_____

_____

_____

_____

_____

_____

_____

How I felt about sex today from my experiences are:

_____

_____

_____

_____

_____

_____

_____

_____

Describe any heavy emotion or feeling:

_____

_____

_____

_____

_____

_____

_____

_____

_____

Where in the body is this feeling felt?

_____

When was the first time (age) that this feeling in that area was felt?

_____

_____

_____

_____

_____

_____

_____

What happened?

_____

_____

_____

_____

_____

_____

_____

_____

What was the positive feeling needed at that time?

_____
_____
_____
_____
_____
_____
_____
_____
_____
_____

How I would like to feel about sex and intimacy is:

_____
_____
_____
_____
_____
_____
_____
_____
_____

Write down the lower feelings and the higher feelings.

Lower Feelings	Higher Feelings	Virtues
_____	_____	_____
_____	_____	_____
_____	_____	_____
_____	_____	_____
_____	_____	_____

Let's apply the pivot-and-shift strategy to release the blocked sexual energy to increase the flow of abundance. Revisit each of the childhood experiences from the higher feelings and virtues, and rewrite the event from the higher perspective.

_____

_____

_____

_____

_____

_____

_____

_____

_____

_____

The value you just got from these exercises can be experienced in full at https://dawnacampbell.com/financially-fit

CHAPTER 14

Opposites Attract

One of the best ways to open the seat of creation is through meditation. This will help balance sexual energy, and increase the sexual energy flow to attract and increase the financial flow of prosperity attraction. Have a journal or some paper next to you. After this meditation, record all of the guidance that you may have received to open and strengthen the seat of creation energy center.

Imagine a beautiful, brilliant bright white light at your feet. Allow the white light to enter through the bottom of your feet, moving up the legs, through the hips, and moving up your spine. Allow the kundalini energy to awaken and start to slowly move up. Imagine each energy center opening and is whole, complete, balanced, and clean.

Seat of Creation Meditation

Imagine the root chakra opening to activate your abundance.

As this energy moves up, the sacral opens, bringing in the powerful creative force. Charisma and magnetism is yours. Like a fountain, energy is moving up to the solar plexus, bringing in the joy of creation. Moving through the heart space, the Universal Force of Love opens and activates the divinity within. Moving slowly, the energy opens the throat, bringing in harmony and peace. Allowing the energy to gently rise, it moves through the third eye, bringing clarity to the visions. As it reaches the crown, a knowingness takes over. Allow the white light to move just above your space, encompassing all of you.

Take a deep breath. Allow the light to expand outside of you in many directions.

With every breath you take, keep expanding.

With a thought, allow your consciousness to effortlessly float down inside of you through the crown, floating as soft as a feather. Moving down, down, down, through the heart, down through the solar plexus, down to the sacral energy center, just behind the belly button.

Sit in your seat of creation. Talk to your energy center. Tell your center how you feel. Ask your center to share with you. Allow the guidance to come through. Ask the sacral any questions that you may have regarding your creations. What is needed for me to move forward? How can I create more abundance in my life? What qualities and virtues do I need to activate my center? What traumas do I need to release from my center? How can I have a balanced and whole center?

There are no right or wrong questions. Only that you ask. Take time and listen to the answers.

When you are done, thank your energy center for the guidance that it shared with you. Allow the energy to move down, back through the root, down the legs, and out the bottom of your feet, grounding you back to the earth.

When sacral energy comes into balance internally, the ability to create in the world magnifies. The internal balance happens when two opposites come together to create a balancing point. This is considered an internal sacred marriage between two opposites, or duality. Through the center point that connects the two, purposeful creation can happen.

Duality

Learning takes place through duality. In the hermetic principles, this is called polarity, two opposite ends of a spectrum that can be seen as a contradiction. Some examples:

A -------------------------------------B

Yin/Yang	Hot/Cold	Sun/Moon
Male/Female	Earth/Sky	Up/Down
Father/Mother	Left/Right	Black/White

There is a reason that opposites attract. It is through the understanding of each opposite that the center point can be found and allow the creation to come into existence. Creation takes the polar opposites, blends them together, and produces something new.

Yin and Yang

Within each person, there are masculine and feminine traits within. The masculine qualities are yang, while the feminine qualities are yin. These qualities are how the two hemispheres of the brain work. Independent of gender, a predominate masculine brain or feminine brain can exist.

The feminine qualities are considered the right side of the brain. This includes intuition, nurturing, verbal skills, creativity, music, art, and inspiration. Feminine qualities include the idea center for manifestation and is the emotional brain. The feminine is the internal self, the quiet receptive energy, and the access to the subconscious.

The feminine energy is a place of being-ness and non-action, a place of knowing yourself. Knowing what to manifest and why we want to manifest the idea is the feminine brain.

When too much time is spent in the feminine brain, an internal imbalance can occur. This could be sitting blissed out in a Zen meditation all day, maybe binge-watching movies or playing video games. When the feminine qualities are engaged for too long of a period of time, the body and energy field become stagnant, and taking action becomes unclear. Staying in this state will appear as complete laziness.

The masculine qualities are considered the left side of the brain. These qualities include action, logic, organization, support, ambitiousness and drive. This is the external self giving and doing. This is a linear energy that is analytical and a step-by-step sequential process. These are the action steps that are taken to bring the idea (feminine) to bring into form (masculine).

When the masculine brain becomes imbalanced, rigidness happens. Action is the only course, and the person runs around doing, doing, doing, without stopping to check what they are doing, why they are doing it, and what is being created. Direction and clarity to the doing has disappeared.

Manifesting and Creation Cycle

Manifesting and creation are often used interchangeably, but they are two distinct functions. Manifesting is an internal process and part of the feminine energy, a knowing of what is wanted. Manifesting is considered formless, because the idea hasn't been actualized yet. There is a sending out of energy waves through the energy body and is considered the electric energy of the electro-magnetic being.

Creation is part of the masculine energy and an outward action step taking process that allows the steps to bring the idea into form. This is the magnetic energy of the electro-magnetic energy of the body, attracting back the manifestation in form.

It's Not a Competition

Two principles of the feminine and masculine, of manifesting and creating, work together. Take for example, having a baby. An egg (female) and sperm (male) need to join together to have an infusion of energy to create life. These two components are needed—without one of them, new life doesn't happen. A woman or man can decide that they want to have a child, regardless of how they choose to bring that child into existence, the counterpart is still needed. You need both ingredients for an infusion. This is the same for the manifestation and creation cycle. It is a fusion of energy. Creation does not happen without first an idea. The idea can't come into form with the manifestation. The manifestation can't come into form without taking action.

CHAPTER 15

Internal Balance

To have an internal balance, the two opposites have a center point. Think of a teeter-totter. One person is on each end, and in the center is the pivot balancing point. This is tri-ality, meaning, a third center point to balance two sides.

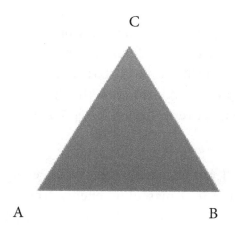

With every two sets of opposites, there is a third point that is between.

Yin/Yang = Wholeness

Hot/Cold = Warm

Father/Mother = Child

Masculine/Feminine = Balance

Earth/Sky = People

Up/Down = Center

Left /Right = Center

Black/White = Grey

Sun/Moon = Stars

When the two opposites come together and meet in the center, a sacred marriage can form internally. That sacred marriage between the masculine and feminine is balanced.

With the feminine qualities, there is the thought, idea, and inspiration on the inside. This is the manifesting stage. Then, with the masculine generating qualities, action is needed to implement the idea into forward movement to the outside world, into the creation stage.

The masculine energy supports the ideas of the feminine energy within. When there is a healthy feminine energy, an idea will start to formulate, and opportunities will start to manifest. It is through the manifestation process of inspiration that ignites the action. The masculine energy takes over with step 1, step 2, step 3... and puts the idea into action.

People often say, "I am always giving". When energy is a giving nature, the person is in a masculine energy. The energy is going outward from the body to share with others. If the person is in the receiving mode, feminine energy is activated, allowing the energy to come inward.

It's Science

The balance between giving and receiving is a frequency of 528 hertz. This is the Universal Force of Love frequency that keeps the giving and receiving in balance and brings wholeness.

Some of the best visionaries of this century were balanced internally, with great insight of ideas that they implemented. Thomas Edison, Nikola Tesla, Steve Jobs, and other leaders were in touch with the feminine qualities of inspiration they wanted to bring into the world. Then, through the balanced masculine qualities, these ideas were brought into existence for the benefit of everyone.

This balance can be in different proportions and not necessarily equal or 50/50. The proportions can also be different daily. A person might spend a few days developing and formulating an idea, and then take action over the next several weeks. However, the masculine energy does need to check in with the feminine energy on a regular basis to ensure that it stays the course to the manifesting idea.

The objective here is to avoid staying one-sided for too long. The closer to the 50/50 balance, the closer to more focus and peace. The challenge is to listen to the intuitive feminine voice inside the head for the guidance before taking those action steps.

Balance and Counter-Balance

Imbalance happens when the masculine energy is action-oriented and doing without checking in with the feminine to understand why it is doing what it is doing. The masculine energy is designed to support and bring into creation the feminine ideas, and if there is not a regular check-in, then the whole project that is manifested can be completely off-course from the original idea. It is important to check in with the feminine for direction on a regular basis.

Partnerships

In partnerships, whether marriage, same-sex partners, or business partners, one person tends to have a predominate masculine brain, while the other has a predominate feminine brain. Not every man has a masculine brain and not every female has a feminine brain. Some men are incredibly right-brained, while women can have a very dominant left brain.

With internal balance in each person, in a relationship, whether personal or business, then externally, each partner can come together and have the ability to shift back and forth to counterbalance the partner. This is how balance in the outside world is created. Partners naturally come together for the balance of these qualities.

If both partners are in the feminine brain too long, the relationship will lack drive and will have lots of chaos in it. The relationship will lose its flexibility and will lack direction moving forward. Basically, the partners are at a standstill. If both partners are in the masculine brain too long, there is a lack of nurturing, and neither partner is getting their needs met. There is constant rigidness, friction, and stubbornness in the relationship with both wanting to implement something. With an internal balance in each person, if you are in a relationship whether personal or business, then externally, each partner can come together.

Paradigm Shift

Traditional roles of the past were based on gender for the role assigned. For example, the man would go out and hunt for food, and the woman stayed back with the children gathering. This is also true throughout this century as well. The man went out to work, and the woman stayed home with the children. This was the norm for a root-based chakra society for survival. In the traditional role, the woman would support the man as he went out and worked. When he returned home, the woman had cooked the meal, and he was served.

As evolution and different liberation movements happen, there has been a shift from these traditional roles for survival to emotional-based society. Today, it takes two people now to support a family. Rather than the roles being assigned by gender, roles are now assigned based on the strength of the masculine and feminine brain patterns, regardless of what the gender is. This is part of the paradigm shift.

The paradigm shift comes first as an individual and happens when a person stops looking outside of themself to feel validated, completed, and whole. The acknowledgement is that everything, including the answers, are inside of you. Turning towards the feminine energy first, the masculine energy will support the ideas in an outward action.

The second paradigm shift happens in a partnership. This is when two people come together in the context of a personal or professional relationship and can shift the roles back and forth. Whomever is in the masculine energy is taking the action steps to support and implement the ideas of the person in the feminine energy. These roles will tend to switch back and forth in a balanced state when used properly. This means that each partnership can ebb and flow, shift and change regularly because the internal balance is supporting each other.

The Balance Point

The balance point between the feminine and masculine is the heart energy center. The perfect frequency of the heart vibration is 528 hertz. This is considered a Solfeggio frequency that the monks chant, and when all the numbers are added together, it adds to a six. The Fibonacci sequence, 3-6-9, is the master sequence in understanding the universe to create anything. The number six is the universal language of love. This frequency is also the bridge that must be crossed to allow the manifestation to become creation.

Albert Einstein's most famous equation is $E=MC^2$. E = energy, M = mass, times the speed light, squared, which creates matter. In his letter to his daughter, Einstein said:

"To give visibility to love, I made a simple substitution in my most famous equation. If instead of $E=MC^2$, we accept that the energy to heal the world can be obtained through love multiplied by the speed of light squared, we arrive at the conclusion that love is the most powerful force there is, because it has no limits."

Love is formless, but forms all things. As human beings, we are both formless and form. There is a spirit or soul that is a wave, an energy that is unseen, the dream world, the divine feminine manifesting energy. As form, there is the physical body that is particles made of matter, that can be seen, and is the divine masculine bringing into creation. Although love cannot always be seen as an energy vibration, we do see the physical forms through symbols: a red rose, a heartfelt hug, or a genuine smile. The doorway to access this unlimited energy of love and to bring into form are faith, trust, and belief.

Love is Formless But Forms all Things

Formless	Form
Waves	Particles
Energy	Matter
Unseen	Seen Thoughts/Feelings Actions
Being	Doing
Divine Feminine	Divine Masculine
Dream World	Physical World
Soul/Creator	Body/us Manifesting Creating

Faith, trust, and belief are needed to access the Universal Force of Love to bring the formless idea into tangible form. The energy of love in the pure, raw form is everything, and anything before it comes into form. It is omnipotent and omnipresent. With direction, you can harness and focus this energy to create instantaneously.

CHAPTER 16

The Pain/Pleasure Cycle

One of the greatest blocks to manifesting and creating is the pain/pleasure cycle. This is a conditioned mind thought form that says pleasure can only come after pain, suffering, sacrifice, or hurt. This is not conscious on our part, but rather subconscious from all the conditioned mind thoughts and beliefs that were experienced in life.

When the first heartbreak happened, love was registered as painful and hurt. In the subconscious, this file gets fed and every time love does not return in the way that was expected, the subconscious registered it as pain. Feeding this file several times creates a pattern that when there is love, there is pain. Followed by after pain comes love. This becomes a vicious loop, and it is hard to break the pattern.

Feeling Good

Pleasure can come in all forms. It can be money, material items, or sex, but the most sought-after commodity that is always on the market is love. This thought/feeling pattern happens when there is low self-esteem or beliefs of not feeling worthy or enough. Through past generations, it was taught that if pleasure was to be experienced, it wasn't given freely, and there was a price to pay, especially hard work. Growing up, some phrases that I heard often were, "no pain, no gain" and "no pain, no glory", enforcing the pain/pleasure cycle.

Attention-Seeking Behavior

Attention-seeking behavior is another way to enforce the pain/pleasure cycle. This is an unusual and negative way for getting emotional needs met. Rather than verbalizing and expressing what is wanted, the emotional needs are acted out, instead. A person might be upset, angry, or extremely frustrated in the heat of the moment and walk off, slamming every door possible to get the other person's attention for them to recognize that there is displeasure. Then, of course, pain is caused internally. This is indicative of a direct need for emotional nurturing that has not been met yet. Attention-seeking behavior is usually taught by parents or other caregivers and can be considered a form of self-abuse. This is another way for emotional pain to be fed internally, enforcing the belief that love is painful or hurtful. The fear is that if words were used, they would not be heard or negative words and actions would be returned instead. Rather than having the pain inflicted from an external source, the negative non-verbal communication is a way to inflict the pain first. The false belief is that you are safe from the other person.

Attachment/Expectation Cycle

The connection with love becomes lost when an imbalance occurs with the manifestation/creation cycle. This brings about the attachment/expectation cycle. Attachment to a particular outcome starts with creating an expectation. Attachment is continually seeking externally to feel something that is wanted or needed on the inside. Attachment is a way to fill the void inside if something feels like it is missing and there is an expectation of return in a predefined way. This cycle limits the Universe in bringing what was asked for because of a preconceived idea or notion that it was to be a certain way. This happens all the time. Money is invested, a return on investment is expected, creating an attachment of performance. A new business venture is created, opportunities come, and there is an attachment and expectation to the success of the business. Attachments to love can even be formed in wanting and expecting that soulmate relationship.

To move out of the attachment/expectation cycle, connection is needed to the Universe and with people. The connecting energy for the Universe is the Universal Force of Love, and to connect with other people, the highest form of connection. Connection and attachment are opposites. Attachment is a needy, clingy energy that can be draining of energy, feeling victimized, or creating a false expectation of gain or return. Connection forms a bond in a relationship with another person, animal, environment, or situation. When the connection is formed from love, there is stability and security. Attachment is a negative connection.

Detachment is releasing any preconceived idea or expectation. Detachment allows the Universe complete freedom to bring the manifestation in form with all possible outcomes. Think about the game of tug-of-war. There are two teams on each side of the rope, pulling. The objective is to pull the other team over the line, but often in the process, the team falls down. This is what happens when attachment to the outcome brings an expectation. Rather than letting go of the end of the rope, we energetically tightly hold on to it, pulling against the Universe, and we are the ones who fall. The manifestation doesn't return, because there was not full detachment in how to receive the manifestation. The Universe is limited in how to bring the request, when it has all wisdom and knowledge that there might be a better way. If the end of the rope was released, detachment happens, and the Universe can bring even faster what was manifested. This is a release of energy to create out in the world, and is naturally the hardest step in manifesting and creating.

Create it Now

In financial planning, there is a goal-setting strategy session with the clients. What are the monetary goals that the client wants to achieve? Is providing for the children's college education important? What about life insurance and disability "just in case" something happens? Is there a strategy to save for retirement? Although this process is a great start, expectations are then created based on external circumstances that are beyond any one person's control. If this process was taken a few steps further and understanding why the client has certain goals, what would happen if the goals were achieved, or not achieved, would allow for the internal success of the client.

When you manifest, the first step is to know what we want to create. Without the ideas and inspiration, the action steps that are needed become unclear. I keep a manifesting-creation notebook. As spontaneous ideas occur, I write them down. I also write down action steps that are needed to create the idea into form.

From Wishing to Manifesting

Let's say I want to travel to Norway and see the Northern Lights. I write down the idea and then include details. Who am I with, what time of year do I go, how long will I be gone for, will I want to do other things in Norway, and do I have friends nearby that I would like to see?

Then, I would start writing down the action steps, such as looking up airline fare, hotels, places to watch the lights, car rentals, and clothing needed. The subconscious will start working on putting the plan together for the experience to come to life.

The goal is to have over 300 manifestations on the list and described in detail. This may sound overwhelming, but the subconscious is very powerful when the blocks and vices have been released. When the blocks are cleared, the subconscious needs a job description. Rather than have the subconscious create old patterns in different ways, the manifesting/creating cycle can be used to give it new instructions. As items come into form and are completed, cross them off, and add more. The idea is to allow the subconscious to work for, rather than against, you.

You can implement these teachings with our financially fit exercises at https://dawnacampbell.com/financially-fit

It's all about finding any lower feelings and then applying the pivot-and-shift strategy. You can then change the lower feelings into the higher to reprogram the energy fuel in the subconscious to have it work for you creating your desires.

CHAPTER 17

Purposeful Creation

The significant step between writing down the manifestations and the action steps is to come into wholeness and balance through the heart center, the Universal Force of Love. This is the center balancing point between the feminine and masculine energy. There are five simple steps to follow and start creating instantly on purpose.

True Intention

The first step is to have and hold a conscious thought form. This is having a knowing of something that is desired to manifest for. This can be anything; a new house, a new car, additional income, or the love of your life. When we hold the conscious thought, it opens up our crown chakra and brings in the gift of claircognizance, "clear knowing".

The first step is to clearly know what it is that you would like to create. Just by knowing what you want to create, the probability will come into existence about 30 to 40 percent of the time, just by holding the thought.

See it to Believe it

Second is to bring in visualization. This allows the thought form to be seen and activates the third eye with the gift of clairvoyance, or "clear seeing". When this energy center is engaged, the imagination is engaged.

When visualizing, make sure that you see yourself in the visualization also. Imagining, daydreaming, and visualizing accesses the alpha brain waves naturally, and this is considered a dynamic meditation. Using this technique of visualizing increases the manifestation coming into existence up to 50 to 60 percent, almost doubling the probability of the thought form to come into existence.

Your Words Know the Way

The next step is having the ability to speak the creation. The throat is the bridge between feeling in the heart and thinking with the brain. By speaking the creation out loud, creation starts to come into existence. Speaking the manifestation out loud activates the gift of clairaudience, or "clear hearing".

When the words are spoken, we hear ourselves speak, and this starts forming the creation into the physical world. Make sure to speak as if the manifestation is already in physical form in the present tense. Affirming that this is in my life today. By adding the words spoken out loud, the probability increases to 70 to 80 percent.

Getting closer to instant thought creation, step #4 will bring the probability up to about 80 to 90 percent with charging the manifestation with a positive feeling. Imagine feeling as if the manifestation was in full physical form today.

This opens up the gift of clairsentience, which means "clear feeling", and it activates the heart center. When the heart center is activated, the energy body magnetically attracts back the very manifestation almost instantly. The frequency sent out of the heart space and body will return as a gravitational force.

Finish Strong

The last step is the most valuable step and is the secret to instantly creating and is all about going deeper. In this last step, the first four steps are combined together, and we stay in the energy until everything disappears and becomes the energy of no thought. There is not any seeing, feeling, or experiencing the manifestation anymore. In this state, there is only sensations that activate the theta brain wave, and is a form of transcendental meditation.

Having no thought allows full detachment from the energy, permitting the Universe with freedom to create. Detachment is a vital step in the process, increasing the probability another 10 to 15 percent, bringing the full percentage to near 100 percent instant thought form creation.

Some Tips

The time that it takes to fully detach the thought will vary by person. Take the time practicing every day. The more practice, the faster instant thought energy creation can happen. Every day, choose something different.

Repeating something that was already manifested for will show the Universe the attachment that still needs to be released. If this process is used daily for one entire year, there will be 365 new creations. If the manifestation didn't return the creation within a reasonable time, there can be a block of energy somewhere in the subconscious that is preventing it from coming into reality.

If this is the case, follow the steps in the earlier chapters to release the block and recharge with the virtue.

Instant Thought Form Creation

Every person has the ability to allow the thoughts to instantly form. The best way to accomplish instant thought form creation is to be in complete alignment with the energy frequency that is emitting from the subconscious and body energy field to what the request is. The pathway is through the Universal Force of Love. Once all lower feelings are released, and all that remain is love and virtues, the request can be sent out to the Universe to magnetically bring it into creation.

Thought Form Energy Creation

Take several deep breaths, breathing in through the nose, out through the mouth. Relax every cell of your body. Take another great big breath in and back out. I want you to imagine that there is a brilliant golden-white light coming in the top of your crown chakra. Moving down through your body, your head, your neck, down your arms, and out your fingers. Down through your heart space, to your torso. This brilliant golden-white light going down your legs, knees, down through the bottoms of your feet. I want you to imagine that this brilliant golden-white light that is radiating through your body extends out in all directions at least six feet.

Next, think of the thought of what you would like to create in your life. Feel the energy of your creation. Next, speak what you would like to create out loud, using your voice. As you speak it, and hold the intent of your thought, visualize that it is already in your life today. Feel the energy, feel the happiness, the joy, the peace, and the calmness that it brings you. Feel that sensation inside of you. Allow that sensation that is inside of you to radiate throughout what you are wanting to create.

This is the energy that attracts what you are asking for into your life. Now, go deeper, into the feeling and the sensation of what you are asking for, until the energy of the thought of the creation disappears. Go deeper. Deeper. Deeper in the energy. Start to only feel your physical space. Feel your breath. You might feel the air all around you. Go deeper. The deeper you go, the more you detach. As you detach, the energy is free to move to create, to bring back to you everything that you are asking for. Go deeper.

With every breath in that you take and with every breath out, go deeper. When you feel that it is just the energy vibrations, you know that you have completely detached the energy. Know that it is done and completed. When you are ready, you take a breath in through your nose, out through your mouth, and open your eyes.

Coming into vibrational alignment with the divine feminine energy for manifesting and allowing the divine masculine energy to take the action steps, we become financially fit, creating on purpose with the Universal Force of Love.

CHAPTER 18

Money is Just Energy

You are energy. Money is energy. Simple.

The Universe does not know the difference between describing the soul energy or money energy. The frequency of the words that describe both money and the soul are the same frequencies. The fuel that charges the frequency of the words is the feeling vibration that is felt.

Super Glue

When the subconscious associates the event and memory, the feeling is the binding agent that holds the frequency in place. When the feeling is shifted to a different one, the whole pattern can change.

How you feel about yourself internally on a subconscious level is how you feel about all the essences in the world around us. As a vibrational being, those feelings and thoughts leave our energy body and form the world around us.

This is how two children can grow up in the same family and have two completely different experiences. This happens because each child is a different vibration and creates different experiences from their perspective filter.

Setting Expectations

There are expectations that money does certain things, like bringing freedom. Money only responds back with the energy and feeling that is applied to it, just like the environment. Money cannot do anything by itself, unless there is meaning applied. Money does not bring freedom, unless freedom is the energy that you assigned to money through vibration and frequency.

If there is not a sense of freedom inside in the essence, then in the environment outside, there will not be a sense of freedom to experience, including freedom around money. The experiences in the world around you are created by the feelings that you have on the inside to create those experiences. This lack of freedom feeling will continue to generate and keep a feeling of limitation, regardless of the amount of money in the account.

Money is a form of energy exchange. This energy that we exchange or trade for what we want and need. In the past, we exchanged silver, gold, land, crops, and animals. Investments were barns, grain for feed, and seed for sowing the fields. Today, we exchange through paper and coin currency of mixed metals, and digital currency as such credit cards, electronic banking, and Bitcoin.

Recognize Scarcity to Stay Abundant

Where the breakdown happens is thinking that money is the life force energy. When money is received, the life force energy fills up, because our energy field is uplifted. When money is spent, the life force energy depletes, because it feels like an expenditure of our personal energy. This model teaches that scarcity with money will create scarcity in the body's energy.

Essentially, how you interact with your finances is how you interact with yourself. The choices of what and when to spend money are solely individual choices. When money is spent, what the money was spent on is also in the energy field.

If the finances and money obligations are all scattered, then it is likely that the energy field is scattered. Since money has an intimate tie to our being-ness, whatever is being produced inside as feelings is also being produced into your personal money supply.

Energy Debts

An expenditure of energy is a debt or obligation. Negative thought forms and feelings spend the body's energy field, while spending money reduces the amount of financial energy resources. When money is spent, the debt obligation also creates a deficit preventing the energy field from becoming whole and complete.

When more is spent than the financial resources on hand, there is an energy debt, both financially and in the energy body. Debt prevents the energy field from becoming whole and complete. When there is debt present, a portion of the energy field can become frozen, then as a result, the money supply can become frozen.

To make matters worse, the money debt is usually paid back with interest, creating even more of a deficit. This debt prohibits the freedom to create, the freedom to have money move fluidly through the Universe and bring abundance.

As the debt clears up and is paid back, money then has the freedom to move and create. Then, a space opens up in the energy body, providing you with the freedom to move and create. The money energy is moving once again, and a surplus can be created, and freedom is restored.

Sometimes, debt is used in order to expand. Through credit, money can be leveraged to create more in business. The debt becomes temporary in nature. Most consumer debt is not from leveraging, but from purchases, usually from income not being sufficient to cover expenses.

Leveraging is one way the financial world operates, but with the energy body, an inverse can happen. Expanding and leveraging financially can put holes and tears into the personal energy supply. The energy field is expanding, to create more, often leaving it depleted and exhausted to make up for the energy deficit for expanding. When the financial gains return's surpluses, the holes in the energy field start to replenish.

Depleting Money Energy

Money has only the meaning that was applied to it. Each person can apply a different meaning based on the beliefs, programs, and feelings from childhood through parents and people who assisted in raising us. These phrases shaped our identity to live by. Children are usually innocent in their request for money and a belief that money will bring back joy and abundance in purchasing things. However, there was implication that if money was spent on the child, this was a "taking", and repayment of some form was expected in return.

Here are common money phrases taught from different cultures during childhood:

* *We can't afford that.*

> This phrase is showing that money is a commodity and scarce. There is not enough money, and there is not any extra. With the personal energy exchange with money, this belief system also indicates a lack of extra money is a lack of extra personal energy,

and the energy body cannot afford the extra. The energy is already depleted.

* *This is my money.*

This phrase is about ownership of money and ignites an energy of hoarding, greed, or jealousy. These vices are consuming. A person with this type of belief system is saying, "I need to keep everything for myself and hoard, because there is not enough for me and you." This belief will also deplete their personal energy field while attempting to stay full, over full, through the accumulation of extra money. If a person is not willing to share in the extra, the supply of money coming to them will cease to flow.

* *Who is going to pay for that?*

This subconscious phrase indicates that sharing of the money supply is not currently possible. Children are taught and expected to share. When a request is made for a sharing of money, it is often confusing to the subconscious with the denial of the request. Often, the child is left feeling unworthy, unimportant, and undervalued. There is confusion between being taught to share and what is experienced. Later as adults, this pattern repeats.

* *Being wealthy is not our destiny.*

The implication here is that wealth will never happen, and the being poor is the destiny. This is in direct conflict with the abundance and prosperity that the Universe has to offer as a divine being. Wealth affects more than just money. Wealth can be in spirit, with love, or in good health.

* I am not rich.

This is a similar belief to not having wealth. Being rich is about more than money. You can be rich in spirit, rich with friends, rich with kindness. Claiming the lack will create lack in all areas of your life. When this lack is acknowledged, our energy field constricts, and the richness of life does expand.

You can implement these teachings with my Financially Fit program at https://dawnacampbell.com/financially-fit

CHAPTER 19

Building Our Energy Supply

Having more money flow in life only requires achieving a vibrational balance with the internal thoughts. Offering a negative internal vibration and expecting money to flow in is a direct conflict. Negativity does not increase abundance and prosperity, but decreases it.

Working on Your Words

If there is doubt, that it is wrong to have money, or if simply there is anger, vibrational alignment with money to bring balance and harmony has not been achieved.

This is how the Law of Attraction works. Like energy attracts like energy. Diamonds cut diamonds. If a poor mental vibration is offered, poorness will attract back. If a rich mental vibration is offered, riches return. A poor mental vibration does not attract riches. These are opposite, dualistic energies that compete.

A negative vibration, thought, or feeling condenses the energy field. Even thinking a word such as tired, anxious, overwhelmed will start to shrink the energy field and will send out the lower vibrations automatically to have that vibration return. A positive vibration, thought, or feeling will expand the energy field.

Words such as kindness, gratitude, and joy will attract those good things back in life. When feeling good, the goodness attracts back in life, including money. This is how to build the personal energy supply to build the external money supply.

A Victory Vibration

What happens when a poor vibration is being offered and a rich vibration is desired? Applying the pivot-and-shift strategy is what it takes. The two are opposite ends of the spectrum, and by applying Newton's three laws of motion, the vibration being offered can change.

In summary, Newton's first law states that an object stays at rest or in motion until it is compelled to change by an external force. The second law is the calculation of how much force is needed to make the object change direction, which needs to be equal or greater than to change. The third law states that for every action, there is an equal and opposite reaction.

Using these laws on a spiritual level, we can take the vibration of a feeling, find the opposite, and meet the original vibration with a force slightly greater than and create the vibrational change. In the example, if there is a poor vibration offered, the counter is meeting that frequency greater with the rich vibration.

Becoming Money

I thought I knew what money was when I was a financial advisor. Over time, I realized that I really didn't. Learning to be a financial advisor didn't necessarily mean that I was qualified to become money. I had only learned some skills. Taking a seminar to learn a healing method doesn't qualify you to become a healer without embracing the experience.

Life is applying the things that are learned in life and fully embracing them. Taking a class, seminar, or workshop to learn a skill is not embracing life.

Here is the difference. I wanted to learn meditation. I read some books, listened to some tapes, practiced what I learned every night, and even took a class with a Zen Buddhist Monk. I only learned meditation. Monks talk about a walking meditation, meaning that everything in life is a meditation, regardless of the activity. To apply this, I moved and lived in an Ashram for a year, embracing the lifestyle to become meditation.

Meditation is not something that I do, but live in every moment. To become anything in the world, you must practice.

Money Energy

Being in the financial services industry qualifies to learn about money. To fully embrace becoming money, the right vibrational mix needs to happen inside to effortlessly attract it in your life. The experiences people have to learn about money depleted the energy supply, personally and monetarily. The best way to come into alignment with the right vibrational mix is to first understand the direct correlation of energy through some common expressions.

Another Type of Self-Fulfilling Prophesy

When a common expression is heard or repeated enough times, the subconscious will start creating a personal truth around it. This happens frequently with money energy. Growing up, the most popular expression I heard was, "Money doesn't grow on trees."

My parents were attempting to teach me and communicate how to be mindful about money. Their desire for me was to spend wisely, be cautious, not overspend, and learn that lavish luxury was not a necessity. This perspective came from their own experiences with money growing up right after the Great Depression. What I learned about money from my parents was not in the vibrational mix of the energy of money.

"Money doesn't grow on trees" only engaged my imagination as a child. If money really did grow on trees, instead of leaves, there would be dollar bills. Maybe even a $100 bill tree. Whenever money was needed, you could walk outside and just pluck a few bills off. When there is a deeper look at expression, there is an understanding that money *does* grow on trees, in the form of energy.

With common expressions, replace the word "money" with the word "energy", and see if there is a truth in both expressions. When the phrase appears to be true for the word money, and it becomes untrue with energy, there is a money belief that was learned, making becoming money impossible.

> Money doesn't grow on trees.
> Energy doesn't grow on trees.

When the word money is replaced with energy, the expression is untrue. Energy does grow on trees in the form of leaves, branches, fruit, and flowers. The pure energy that the trees produce can be converted into money energy.

Fruit can be sold, flowers can cut and made into arrangements and sold, and the leaves and other green parts of the trees convert sunlight energy into usable light energy for the health of the body.

Chlorophyll is green pigment that the plants use as energy that can be harvested and made into supplements that we consume for energy, which requires an exchange of energy if purchasing. Plants are consumed for food and nutritional energy, essential oils, and healing herbs.

Money really does grow on trees—perhaps not in the way I imagined as a child. When money changes to the word energy, the right vibrational mix comes together to start becoming money.

Here are other expressions that the word energy can replace the word money.

Money is the root of all evil.
Energy is the root of all evil.

Money is a burden.
Energy is a burden.

Money is a limited resource.
Energy is a limited resource.

I am not good with money.
I am not good with energy.

You have to work hard for money.
You have to work hard for energy.

Money doesn't fall from the sky.
Energy doesn't fall from the sky.

A penny saved is a penny earned.
Energy saved is energy earned.

Money makes people arrogant.
Energy makes people arrogant.

You cannot spend money like water.
You cannot spend energy like water.

Money – easy come, easy go.
Energy – easy come, easy go.

Write down some of the personal money expressions and rewrite the expression using the word energy. This will start aligning the right vibrational mix to become money.

You can implement these teachings with my Financially Fit program at https://dawnacampbell.com/financially-fit

CHAPTER 20

Four Sides to a Quarter

There are four sides to a quarter. Yes, four sides.

Social conditioning recognizes two sides: heads and tails. Mostly because they are the opposite sides used for determination. Flipping a coin at a football game will determine which side goes first or who wins a bet.

Technical Creativity

If there is creativity, the ridge might be the third side. The ridge is the intersecting point between two circles if the image was drawn two-dimensionally. Head, tails, and the side ridge that connects the two sides would overlap. There is always a center balancing point between two opposites and creates the third dimensional world we live in.

The fourth side? This is the space in-between everything, in-between all the matter inside of the quarter that is unseen. If there was a microscope powerful enough, the matter inside the quarter will not be touching.

This in-between space is the essence of the quarter, allowing the quarter to be expressed as a quarter. Even with inorganic matter, there is this space within the density. This is the start of the fourth dimension: understanding that the world is fluid and an expression of the essence of what is inside. The fourth side is an inside-out perspective.

Programming and Reprogramming

This space inside physical matter is programmable. Just as feelings are programmable inside of the energy body as matter, inorganic matter can also be programmed. Money is an external form of energy, and energy is programmable.

Anything that can be done with energy can be done with money. The thoughts and feelings inside of you transmit and are received in the programmable space of money, just like the radio transmitter and receiver. How you think and feel about yourself programs money, the external source of our energy supply.

Programing Money

There are several ways to reprogram money. One way is by changing the feelings on the inside to change and affect the outside world. This has been the focus of *Financially Fit*. Here are some additional tips for programing money.

Program Tip #1:

How do you *want* to feel about money? By uncovering how you want to feel about money, the pivot-and-shift strategy can be used in reverse to match the internal vibration to the external vibration you want. The first step is to create a list of how you want to feel about money.

This is a BONUS section from our workbook and course through my personal coaching program. Use these interactive exercises to reset and reboot your brain for financially fit brilliance.

I want to feel .... about money (circle the favorites and add and additional words)

Abundant	Happy	Safe	Worry-free
Rich	Joyful	Peaceful	Creative
Profitable	Satisfied	Harmonious	Available
Prosperous	Secure	Successful	Balanced
Plentiful	Empowered	Fulfilled	Expansive
Respectful	Capable	Enough	Confident
Carefree	Wise	Purposeful	Judiciously
In Control	Loved	Knowledgeable	

Add in a few of your own words

_____ _____ _____

_____ _____ _____

_____ _____ _____

_____ _____ _____

Once the most important qualities are circled, check and see if the feeling is inside of you.

The positive feeling is _____

_____

I feel this feeling in my body located here _____

_____

The first time I remember feeling this feeling was at age _____

_____

The event that took place was _____

_____

_____

_____

_____

_____

_____

_____

If the positive feeling is not there, then use the pivot-and-shift strategy earlier to bring in the new feeling to start matching how you want the vibration of money to come to you.

Program Tip #2: You can program money as the divine expression of you. We are all divine expressions of the Universal Force of Love energy. As this divine expression, you are complete love. From the inside-out perspective, being complete love will allow money and everything else in life be an extension and expression of this love. Money becomes energy expression of love, allowing for the gratitude for services rendered. Money comes into balance, being plentiful, and shared for products, services, or gifts. Abundance is the divine birth right. Accepting the abundance becomes a simple expression of appreciation of service, a pure symbol of love and integrity.

Program Tip#3: Blessing money with the qualities that are desired. Every time the money is blessed, every person who comes into contact with the money will receive these qualities in the shared energy field. The energy can still be felt on a subconscious level, even if it is paper money, currency coins, or digital.

This is a way to "pay it forward" using money. Holding the intent that the money spent is blessed threefold to return to you and every person who uses the money in the future will also generate prosperity for everyone. Blessing the money will help shift and change the consciousness of others, as everyone is worthy of abundance.

Program Tip #4: When mediation is engaged, there is direct access to the divine energy within and the Universal Force of Love energy that moves through all things. When a meditation practice is used, the spiritual essence transmutes the discord energy into harmony, ignorance into wisdom, fear into love, and lack into abundance. When this energy is transmuted, the higher frequencies attract back even more abundance.

Program Tip #5: Number sequences and repeating number patterns can be used to trigger a reminder to program money. Number patterns can be house numbers, time on a clock, repeating receipt totals, or license plates. These patterns can show up anywhere and can include 111, 222, 333, 12:34, 1:23, $11.11, $99.99.

Maybe there are some favorite sequences. One of my number patterns that show up is 811. Every time a repeating sequence shows up, repeat positive money affirmations. I am abundant, I have plenty to spend, I am a money magnet, I am blessed and can bless others, I vibrate money, I become money, I am in alignment with money. This will assist in attracting more into life to be shared and will help keep the divine flow going.

The Space In-Between

When money is programmed from the inside with intention, money as a vice transitions to a virtue. Abundance is the creative energy in the formless Universal Force of Love and is unseen and invisible. When money becomes visible, the energy is created into form through manifestation and financial energy increases. Becoming money is how to be financially fit, living the life experience to the fullest while reaching vibrational alignment with feelings and thoughts.

Meditation Money Programming

Take a big breath in, and release. Take another big breath in, inhaling through your nose, exhaling through your mouth. Imagine that you are sitting in a brilliant, bright light. Breathe deeply.

Take a deep breath. Hold the intention that all forms of debt you have are with you in the shared energy field and the brilliant bright light. Imagine the debt being infused with the qualities to be paid, easily and effortlessly, blessing the in-between space for the debt to vanish. Qualities of abundance, prosperity, and generosity infuse into the debt, eliminating the financial obligation. Take a few moments and infuse the debt with any other quality you desire to have it eliminated. Hold the intention the debt is paid off three times as fast, bringing in financial harmony for yourself and others.

Hold the intention that all the physical money in dollars and coins that you have are with you in the shared energy field and the brilliant bright light. Imagine the money being infused with the qualities that you want to return to you, blessing all the space in-between. Qualities of abundance, prosperity, and generosity infuse into the physical money. Infusing with joy, happiness, and gratitude for all that touch the money moving forward. Take a deep breath, and allow the energy to infuse. Take a few moments and add in additional qualities you would like to share with the world through the physical form of money. Bring in the qualities of security, appreciation, and accelerated growth and return. Infuse these into the physical money and multiplied for every person and yourself threefold, creating good will and abundance for everyone.

Take a deep breath. Hold the intention that all the digital currency in your accounts that you have are with you in the shared energy field and the brilliant bright light. Imagine the digital currency being infused with the qualities that you want to return to you, blessing all the space in-between. Qualities of abundance, prosperity, and generosity infuse into the digital currency. Infusing with joy, happiness, and gratitude for all that touch the money moving forward. Take a deep breath and allow the energy to infuse. Take a few moments and add in additional qualities you would like to share with the world through the digital form of money. Bring in the qualities of security, appreciation, and accelerated growth and return. Infuse these into the digital money and multiplied for every person and yourself threefold, creating good will and abundance for everyone.

Take a deep breath. Hold the intention that all forms of investments you have are with you in the shared energy field and the brilliant bright light. Imagine the investments being infused with the qualities that you want to return to you, blessing all the space in-between. Qualities of abundance, prosperity, and generosity infuse into investments. Infusing with joy, happiness, and gratitude for all who touch the money moving forward. Take a deep breath and allow the energy to infuse. Take a few moments and add in additional qualities you would like to share with the world through the investment form of money. Bring in the qualities of security, appreciation, and accelerated growth and return. Infuse these into the investments and multiplied for every person and yourself threefold, creating good will and abundance for everyone.

CHAPTER 21

Money Motivation

Money has become more significant over the years than realized. Money has been the external reward for the actions that have been taken in the workforce, making smart investment choices, and for services offered. Social conditioning teaches that money is received for an exchange of labor and talents. Although money can be a motivating factor, the subconscious has different motivations. The subconscious is the true motivating factor when it comes to money generation.

Inspiring Wants and Wishes

Money does provide an exchange for the experiences in life providing for adventure, travel, and vacation time. Money also provides a way to pay financial obligations.

Money does condition the subconscious that there is an exchange of energy for accomplishments, achievements, and talents starting at an early age. Children are rewarded by completing chores teaching the value of money, rewarding hard work, and that to have money, giving is necessary.

Some parents went even further to educate their children about money. The child was rewarded by completing tasks, but spending all of the money was not allowed. Rather than just handing over the money, there was a system, a jar system. One jar was for spending, one jar was for saving, one jar was for charity, and one jar was taxes, which went back to the parents. This did teach about life and how the money system works, but not everyone grew up this way.

My parents expected me to do chores and keep my bedroom clean because I was part of a family. Since I lived there, I was responsible for my part. This conditioned my subconscious that if I wanted money, I needed to get a job, work hard, and pay my own way. At the age of 14, I went into the workforce to have the ability to buy my own clothes, lunch at school, and books that I loved to read. Although I grew up in Silicon Valley, my family was near the poverty line, and to have anything in addition to food and shelter meant I worked.

Lack Motivation

Money can motivate in different ways, and lack is one of them. When there is a need for money, motivation to work, find income, and meet financial obligations become the reason why we go to work. Whether working for someone else or having your own business, work happens. This is one of the reasons why people show up for work every day: the need for money.

What Do You Take Pride In?

Through the stress and worry, health can break down, but still people show up to work to receive a paycheck. If self-employed, the result is similar, showing up because sometimes affording a sick day isn't possible. The next sales call, the next appointment, the next customer is what feeds the family because of the need. People do take pride for never taking a sick day.

When the paycheck is received, feeling abundant and on top of the world brings a euphoric feeling inside. As the money is spent, little is left, depletion sets in, feeling limited in spending, and not being able to move on happens until the next paycheck. Then, the social conditioning subconscious pattern repeats.

Advice Motivation

Being of service to others can motivate anyone in the advice business. Coaches, life mentors, and healers love to see their clients become better. Financial advisors and people in the financial services industry love being of service and assisting their clients reach their money goals. The advice and service industry has desire to help and assist everyone. The reward for being of service is monetary return. In the advice industry, being paid on commission or clients directly paying you is how payment is received for the exchange.

Even on a scheduled day off, if called, people in the advice industry show up as a result of subconscious conditioning that failing to appear will result in no sale. Frustration, feeling worn out, never having personal time, not wanting to answer the phone are all side effects, but yet, the advice coach shows up for the monetary reward. There is a subconscious fear that if a day is taken off, clients will stop calling all together, and the next dollar won't be earned. There is a feeling of obligation to always help the client in every way possible, but the deeper subconscious obligation is to create a monetary return, due to the inherent fear.

It does sound a bit selfish to say that being of service is motivated by money. The subconscious is designed to create and run programs to achieve goals and will use any possible way to keep motivation on life's path, including fear and money.

There is a difference between being of service to someone and being a servant. In the advice industry, often, the client's needs are put before your own needs and the emotional needs of the family. In a servant position, the needs for everyone comes before individual needs and personal needs are always last, if they happen at all. When a person is continually in a servant role, being of service is not possible. The energy is always depleted, giving everything out to have a return of money. Maintaining a balance between service and personal emotional needs being met will keep the subconscious from going into servant mode.

Kindness Motivation

"Kindness is a language which the deaf can hear and the blind can see."
– Mark Twain.

The soul knows that the pathway to happiness is through service. The soul has an inherent desire to help others unconditionally. There is such a strong, deep internal desire to help others. Kindness is how the soul feels connected with others, giving and receiving. To be in service through kindness is a different subconscious motivation and intention. Kindness is an internal motivating factor through love and a heart's desire by doing good deeds. If money is received, it is the icing on the cake.

Kindness wants the world to be a better place and gives a power to improve the well-being of others. Kindness is an expression of graciousness and can be used to inspire employees, make businesses profitable, and creates a ripple effect. Kindness inspires kindness.

There are many benefits to being motivated by kindness. Kindness reduces stress and aging, dropping the cortisol levels and increasing endorphins, increasing pleasure and happiness. As these levels shift in the body, depression and anxiety start to reduce, and motivation happens. Building a kindness muscle is the result and is a part of the natural personality and lifestyle being created. The more kindness that is created, the more the brain rewards with feeling good and motivation to do more. Every outward act of kindness facilitates generosity in return. With kindness, receiving money becomes a side effect, rather than the goal.

Philanthropist Motivation

Philanthropists have a giving commitment with service. People who are motivated by philanthropy have a deep desire to promote the welfare of others and through money donations. Their mindset goes beyond themself as an individual, their family, and their community. This is a global perspective of universal giving. There is a genuine love for people and for all of humanity. Kindness is a part of the philanthropy, but it goes a few steps further.

Philanthropist motivation is about how money can be used for the common greater good of society. This motivation is about changing the hearts and minds of people. The motivation is to create connections through peace, community, and understanding. Generous hearts are a large part of how a philanthropist is motivated.

There is a misconception that to be motivated by philanthropy that you have to have large amounts of money. Philanthropy is a motivational mindset, not a dollar amount. With this mindset, a grassroots cause or organization can be started and soliciting donations of money, time, and energy, which can fund projects. Many of the foundations and organizations that exist today started out as grassroots. As the message was communicated to the people, funding came in, and projects around the world were initiated to help make the world a better place. As the hearts and lives of people are healed, beautiful hearts are created.

Mother Teresa was a true philanthropist in many ways. Although she chose personally to live a life of minimalism, she was in a sense the richest woman on the planet. Mother Teresa had the ability to call up any person she chose and ask for money, and received it for whatever amount she asked for.

Spiritual Motivation

The subconscious is so incredibly smart that money will be used as a means for spiritual growth. Money and finances are used to motivate our human self to stay on a spiritual pathway. The subconscious will create clever ways to keep you motivated and stay on track. This happens when the existing career choice does not feel satisfying anymore. Sometimes, the Universe will add on some additional financial stress, just to keep the spirit moving forward.

Spiritual motivation includes moving forward on the divine path, completely the mission work that the soul came here to learn. When the previous pathway to earning income is not working and the passion is lost, this is the subconscious coming in for a correction.

Leaving the financial services industry was difficult for me. I also knew that I didn't have the passion for it as I once did. There was fear, not knowing how I was going to earn income. Intuitively, I knew that I could not stay the path, because I paid for it with my health, being in the hospital (my first wakeup call), then my relationships ended (my second wakeup call), then I became unemployable in the industry during a global recession and financial devastation happened (my third wakeup call). After I left the ashram, I did attempt to start a new career in financial services as a need to earn income. However, my subconscious and soul knew differently and created outcomes to keep pushing me forward to a new career path. The Universe supported me and has always been providing since.

I have been asked before if I could change anything in the past if I would. My answer is no. I would have chosen to go through all of the same events to have this moment. If any one of those events changed, I would not be here. This is the greatest gift I could give others and myself. During this time, I did make a promise to the Universe to continue the work I started for keeping my children and myself safe. I fulfill that promise every day to the best of my ability.

CHAPTER 22

Funding your Dreams

Money motivation can also come in the form to fund personal dreams. We create from energy, and money and time are forms of energy. Investing in yourself is a way to fund your dreams.

Opportunities are often silent and open the doorways to new business adventures. When the doorway is open, the energy can flow in, assisting the business adventure and create the cash flow that is needed. This is what it feels like to be in divine timing. Everything flows through and fully supports the dreams.

When a new business starts up, others are blessed with jobs. When a new service is offered, someone starts their path to creating and bringing others with them. How many people can benefit when dreams are funded? When those steps are taken to fund dreams, there is a natural love motivation that takes over. Joy and happiness take over when the natural motivation comes in. This becomes a sharing of the natural gifts and talents and how legacies are left.

The Top 50

The top 50 global entrepreneurs were interviewed about money motivation. The question that was asked for each of them was what advice they would give to be successful in business. Here is a summary of their responses:

1.) Have a passion with a driving force.

2.) Love what you do, and you have got to do it.

3.) Emotionally invest in yourself.

4.) Emotionally invest in what you do.

5.) Be an idea generator.

6.) Believe in yourself and others will believe in you.

7.) Foster your dreams, and they will become a reality.

8.) Be an inspiration.

9.) Share through teaching and writing.

10.) Commit to your values.

Every entrepreneur had a different internal motivation to why they choose to create, their subconscious why. Not one perspective even mentioned the word money. They all created to have an internal happiness inside first. After all, happiness is an inside job.

Create your Abundance Story

How every person is motivated becomes a part of the abundance story. When the motivation to create becomes stronger than the financial gain, the financial fortune becomes closer to actualizing.

I have been motivated by all of the different money motivations that are shared here. Personally, for me today, the challenge is to see what can be accomplished for the greater good of all and making the world a better place.

The emphasis isn't so much on creating money anymore as it is to see how the money can be used for to create. This is creating on purpose.

Having an abundance story is a good place to recognize where to start with how you are personally motivated. This gives a starting point to grow, shift, and change from. My abundance story has shifted and changed many times as I grew as an individual.

There was a period of time during which I wanted to give up with my healing career. I wanted desperately to be out and get a job. The hardship came when I did not even have $2.00 at that time to purchase a cup of coffee. I didn't know where the next dollar was coming from, and I was too embarrassed to ask for help. I was committed to getting a job. I had met with a friend that day, and she did not allow me to quit. She believed in me when I couldn't. That day, she wrote me a check in advance for teaching children about spirituality and healing, and told me that I was going to teach a week-long summer camp for them. I will never forget this day.

One of my greatest desires from that day was to start a foundation, called The Healing Heart Foundation, as a way to give back paying it forward. The idea is to believe in people when they are not able to believe in themselves, helping and assisting them move onto their life path. This is a way for me to contribute back to the world that has been so generous with me. Today, that foundation is in existence, and a percentage of the proceeds from this book goes to fund the foundation. This is part of my abundance story.

Your "abundance story" is another really fun and effective method I use when helping people become financially fit. For more information, visit https://dawnacampbell.com/financially-fit

This is how we truly become financially fit in all areas of life, health, wealth, and relationships, to create happiness, prosperity, and love in the world around us.